Teachers and the Law
A Practical Guide for Educators

A. Wayne MacKay
and
Lyle I. Sutherland

1992
EMOND MONTGOMERY PUBLICATIONS LIMITED
TORONTO, CANADA

Printed in Canada.

Produced by WordsWorth Communications of Toronto, Canada using Author/Editor® and PageMaker® on the Apple® Macintosh™ computer. Camera-ready pages produced on the LaserMAX 1000™.

Canadian Cataloguing in Publication Data

MacKay, A. Wayne, 1949 –
    Teachers and the law : a practical guide for educators

ISBN 0-920722-43-1

1. Teachers – Legal status, laws, etc. – Canada.
2. Students – Legal status, laws, etc. – Canada.
I. Sutherland, Lyle I.   II. Title.

KE3805.S88 1992   344.71'07   C92-095085-X
KF390.E3S88 1992

27.²²

This book is dedicated to Alex MacKay, who volunteered many hours as Chair of the Pictou County School Board, and Evaline MacKay, who provided a model of caring education in the home.

And to Lyle Sutherland (Sr.) and Mary Sutherland, who have both dedicated their professional careers to children and education.

Table of Contents

Acknowledgments

This book would not have been possible were it not for the assistance of many people. First and foremost we would like to thank the teachers, administrators, and school board officials across the country who invited us to lecture in their area and thereby provided the exchange of ideas and issues that form the basis of this work.

We are indebted to Trudy Moore, who courageously endured the typing of the first draft, and Pauline Rooney, who sifted through the mounds of revisions, above and beyond the call of duty. Siobhan Lane and Jeff Christen provided some very helpful legal research when it was most needed.

We are also thankful for the friendly, patient, and "flexible" staff at Emond Montgomery who worked and reworked timetables to accommodate two busy lawyers.

Last, but certainly not least, thanks to Phil and Nancy Murlee, and "J.C." Cameron, who generously provided their cabin on the shores of the Northumberland Strait in Arisaig, Nova Scotia, where the bulk of the first draft was put together.

A. Wayne MacKay
Lyle I. Sutherland

Introduction

The field of education law has expanded rapidly over the past decade. Although this expansion may present a new and exciting challenge for many lawyers and educational administrators, it has largely represented a troublesome development for teachers. While educational issues have traditionally been handled at the political level through provincial departments of education and local school boards, the arrival of the Canadian Charter of Rights and Freedoms in 1982 signalled a change. Judges and lawyers have now become significant players in the shaping of educational policy.

Teachers are perhaps the most important component in any educational structure. When the classroom door is closed, the responsibility for educating today's children rests squarely on their shoulders. In spite of their vital role in the proper functioning of the educational system, teachers have traditionally been victimized by outdated expectations with regard to their legal roles and responsibilities both in and out of the classroom. The emergence of education law issues in the last 10 years has only created more confusion for teachers.

The law generally can be mystifying. Historically, lawyers and judges have not made the necessary efforts to demystify the law and legal process. Lawyers are often guilty of resorting to legal jargon instead of using plain language to explain legal principles. Through the numerous lectures and in-services that we have conducted across the country, we have been able to gain, to some extent, a better understanding of the mysteries of the law as seen through the eyes of teachers. Although there is a trend toward teachers and administrators writing legal handbooks for teachers, we think it is important that lawyers provide this information. Some of the issues involved, such as constitutional law, are very complex and are best explored by lawyers. Lawyers must make a greater effort to address the issues from a teacher's viewpoint, rather than from a legal perspective.

As the field of education law has grown and become more complex, so too have the roles and responsibilities of teachers. Rather than explore legal issues in the traditional legal framework of negligence, criminal law, labour law, etc., we have divided this book into chapters that focus on these roles and responsibilities, with the legal issues woven into the discussion.

Before embarking on our exploration of these roles, we will first take a brief tour through the legal system in Canada, highlighting the areas that touch upon education. We will also look at the actual role and status of a teacher as seen through the eyes of the law.

Constitutional Basis of School Law

Our Canadian constitution (as of 1982) is divided into essentially two parts: the Constitution Act, 1867 and the Constitution Act, 1982. The 1867 constitution sets out a list of exclusive federal powers in section 91 and a list of exclusive provincial powers in section 92. Examples of this division of powers occur in our daily lives. The federal government has exclusive authority over matters such as banking, national defence, criminal law, patents, navigation and shipping, and aboriginal peoples. The provinces have jurisdiction over matters of a "merely local or private nature," "property and civil rights," and particular items such as the court system, hospitals, and municipal governments.

Education has historically enjoyed special status because it is identified by a separate section in the Constitution Act, 1867. Section 93 specifically assigns the legislative authority over education to the provinces. They are exclusively permitted to make laws that relate to education, subject to certain protections for denominational schools. For this reason, education has long been considered the "jewel" of the provinces and there has historically been very little federal interference in the educational sphere. One exception to this rule is the federal jurisdiction over education with respect to Indians and the residents of the Yukon and Northwest Territories.

In recent years, the most important constitutional development in education law has been the entrenchment of the Charter of Rights and Freedoms as part of the Constitution Act, 1982. The Charter, as part of the constitution, is the "supreme law of Canada" and any legislation that is inconsistent with it is inoperative. We will examine the various aspects of the Charter as they relate to education throughout this book. In general terms, one of the most dramatic effects of the Charter is that it is leading toward national standards in education.

Prior to the enactment of the Charter, education (other than denominational schools) was strictly within the realm of the provinces, and educational rights and privileges were defined by the provincial education acts. Even with respect to the Indians and residents of the North, the federal educational jurisdiction was largely delegated to the provinces and local territorial councils. There was also considerable power left in the hands of local school boards. The Charter, however, establishes rights and freedoms for every Canadian citizen regardless of his or her residence. As the courts hear cases that involve the impact of constitutional rights on education, the provinces are being forced to adjust their legislation to comply with the norms of the Charter. Ontario must now pay attention to what the courts are saying in Alberta and Nova Scotia (and vice versa) if it hopes to avoid similar challenges in its own courts. Although education is a provincial matter, there is now a nationalizing influence in the form of court decisions on the Charter.

Specific School Law Sources

There are various levels of school law sources, each with differing levels of scope and legal force. The Charter has the strongest possible legal force and widest possible scope. However, it touches on only certain aspects of education law. With the exception of denominational school rights (section 29) and minority language education rights (section 23), the provisions of the Charter are not aimed specifically at education.

The provinces provide the most comprehensive sources of education law through their respective education statutes. These statutes codify the law of the province and cover most aspects of administration from the powers and responsibilities of the minister of education to the duties of pupils. They define school districts and outline the powers and duties of school boards, teachers, and principals. Although provincial statutes deal with similar subjects, their widely varying approaches reflect the unique historical development of each province.

In addition to the education acts of each province, there are statutes that regulate specific aspects of education.[1]

A second source of law created by the provinces is known as "subordinate legislation" or "regulations." These are expressly authorized by a section of the education act and may be passed by the minister of education or the Cabinet without a vote by the members of the legislature. Regulations carry the same legal force as a statutory provision but are usually more detailed and technical in scope. Regulations are attractive to governments as a means of implementing education policies with the full force of law, without having to debate the issue in the legislature. The minister and the provincial Cabinet are given a broad power to make regulations affecting many aspects of education in all of the provincial school statutes.

The next step down in the legal hierarchy is the bylaws or policy manuals implemented by school boards. These are guidelines that school administrators and school boards may enact to govern their own activities, but they normally carry little weight in a courtroom. In other words, a parent may complain to a school board that a certain school policy is not being followed; however, this will rarely in and of itself serve as a basis for legal action. A policy may have legal force if it can be tied to one of the other sources of law.

The final major source of education law in Canada is the common law, or "judge-made" law. This body of law is based on the decisions of judges who hear cases across the country, and is in a constant state of evolution. As parents have become more familiar with protections afforded by the Charter, there has been a surge of judge-made law in the field of education. Some commentators have dubbed this phenomenon a new "rights consciousness" on the part of parents. Judges are therefore becoming prominent figures in the field of education, and this is likely to continue until the provinces fully adapt their education policies to reflect the newly protected rights and freedoms entrenched in the Charter.

Related Sources of Education Law

Education touches many aspects of our lives, and, consequently, is affected by many different and related sources of law. Not the least of these sources is the criminal law, which has undergone significant changes over the past decade. The entire juvenile justice system was overhauled in 1984 through the creation of the Young Offenders Act — an act that has radically changed the way children are dealt with in the legal system. The Criminal Code was amended in 1988 to better protect children from sexual abuse, and these broad protections have caused a great deal of concern among teachers. Although teachers are concerned about the welfare of their students, they must also be aware of the danger of falling victim to damaging allegations of physical or sexual abuse.

As the workplace becomes more complex, labour law has also proved to be an important area of law for teachers. In most provinces, the labour relations of teachers are regulated by distinct collective bargaining legislation. The major difference between these statutes and general labour legislation is the limitation on the right to strike found in the teachers' collective bargaining acts.

Copyright law has also emerged as a concern for teachers in the form of a new Copyright Act, which does not protect the use of materials for educational purposes. Copyright is within federal jurisdiction and thus affects schools in every province.

Family law issues increasingly arise in schools as governments become more involved in regulating family relationships. There has been a strong movement recently toward detecting and prosecuting child abusers. This trend means that teachers must become more aware of the warning signs of abuse and familiarize themselves with the mandates of local social services agencies. Every province's children's services legislation makes it mandatory to report any suspicion that a child is "in need of protection." A failure to do so can result in prosecution.

These various sources of law will be discussed in more detail as they arise in the context of specific educational issues. Education law is connected to other legal spheres, and to understand it fully, one must have a general appreciation of the larger framework of Canadian law.

Legal Procedures and Related Matters

The legal system in Canada was grafted onto the old British common law traditions and is similar to the legal systems in other Commonwealth countries. The preamble to the Constitution Act, 1867, describes the Canadian governmental system as "similar in principle to that of the United Kingdom." Each province has a "superior court" with an inherent jurisdiction to deal with any form of legal dispute. This superior court level may be broken into a trial division and an appeal division, but in most provinces there is a separate statutory appeal court. There are also "inferior courts" created by statute. These courts (such as Family Court and Small Claims Court) have defined purposes and limited jurisdictions. The final level of appeal is the Supreme Court of Canada, whose decisions are binding on all courts at all levels. The decisions of the various provincial appeal courts are "persuasive," but are not binding outside their province of origin. There are also federal courts of limited jurisdiction, but school issues would be raised there rarely, if at all.

From the perspective of a parent pursuing an education law issue, the road to final resolution is often long and expensive. The first line of attack is to discuss the problem with the relevant school board authorities, and perhaps attend a meeting of the full school board. It is becoming increasingly popular to have lawyers represent the interests of parents at these school board meetings. If there is no satisfaction at this administrative level, then the next step may be to move into the trial division of the superior court of the province and institute legal proceedings. It can take as much as two years to prepare a case for court and complete the trial. Considering the expenses involved, there is a substantial incentive to settle these disputes before going to trial.

If the case is completed at trial, the losing party must decide whether to accept defeat or appeal the ruling. The next step in the litigation process is to the appeal division of the province; the appeal can take up to a year to be heard, depending on the court's schedule. If the case is of national importance, the final route of appeal is to the Supreme Court of Canada. To take a case from trial to the Supreme Court of Canada can take as long as five years and can easily cost in excess of $100,000. This means that courts are not easily accessible to average Canadians.

Legal Role and Status of Teachers

Against this tapestry of interwoven sources of law, we turn now to the status of teachers within this framework. The question of a teacher's legal status has been a neglected issue for many years. Perhaps this explains why the intervention of law into educational policy in recent years has caused such a shockwave throughout the teaching community. Traditionally, teachers have been largely immune from examination under the microscope of the law. However, as the law becomes increasingly involved in education, so too are teachers swept into the legal process.

Ask any teacher who has studied education law what he or she considers to be the role and legal status of a teacher in the classroom, and they will answer, "I stand in the place of a parent for the purpose of teaching children." Ask this teacher what the standard of care in negligence is for teachers and they will answer, "I must exercise the care of a reasonable and prudent parent." Ask the same teacher about the scope of his or her discipline and they will tell you that they are to exercise the discipline of a "kind, firm, and judicious parent." Teachers are inundated with role references based on parental delegation of authority. This is the common law origin of the status of a teacher.

The theory of parental delegation is drawn from the historical doctrine of *in loco parentis*. This is a Latin phrase meaning "in the place of a parent." Historically, this doctrine served as an important basis for a teacher's legal authority. In the early 1900s, for example, parents were often left to their own devices to form a community school board and build their own school. Parents were thus able to prescribe the manner in which their children were to be taught, and they bore the primary responsibility for the hiring and firing of teachers. Most commentators agree that teachers in this era had little privacy or autonomy. Furthermore, the fact that the one-room school contained students from grades 1 to 12 meant that it was possible for the same teacher to teach the same child for 12 years, and for the teacher simultaneously to teach 3 or 4 children from the same family. This is the model of education that existed when many education statutes were first drafted.

Although the doctrine of *in loco parentis* may well have been operative in the early part of this century, it has been eroded almost to the point of extinction in past decades. Although the doctrine still has some life in the common law duties of teachers, it has largely been supplanted by statute.

Without recourse to the developments in the case law, we need only look at the realities of the school setting to realize that *in loco parentis* has little or no place in today's schools. Although the one-room schoolhouse and community school boards may have provided a real setting for parents to delegate their inherent authority to teachers, the post-1960 world of centralized school authority and legislative regulation leaves little room for a similar delegation. Parents are now separated from teachers by a vast maze of administrative and governmental structures. Discretion has been replaced with legislation and regulations that have often left both parents and teachers with a sense of powerlessness.

In addition to *in loco parentis*, teachers, as agents of the state, have also exercised an additional legal role under the common law principle of *parens patriae*. This principle has been defined as follows:

> The sovereign as *parens patriae* has a kind of guardianship over
> various classes of persons who, from their legal disabilities stand in
> need of protection, such as infants, idiots, and lunatics.[2]

The provinces hire teachers in this *parens patriae* capacity to act as state agents for the purpose of providing education to children.

Given that teachers have exercised their role under both the *in loco parentis* and *parens patriae* principles, the question remains: Which of these principles is the primary basis for the present legal status of teachers? Even in the early part of this century, state agency in the form of statutory authority was the predominant basis for teachers' legal authority. This is most clearly seen in the areas of compulsory education and corporal punishment. If a parental delegation were the primary basis for a teacher's authority, then parents should be able to define or revoke that delegation. In cases that involved compulsory education, parents attempted to revoke the delegation of authority to teach their children by refusing to send their children to provincial schools. The reasons for refusing to send children might differ in each case. They were, however, told by the courts in most cases that the government's compelling interest in the education of children should prevail. The role of the state in protecting the child trumped that of the parent.

In cases that involved corporal punishment, parents attempted to "define" their in loco parentis delegation by restricting the use of force on their children. If in loco parentis were the primary basis for a teacher's authority, then a teacher would be liable for civil assault charges where parents have expressly instructed that their child not be touched. As early as 1910, the courts have upheld the statutory role of teachers to use reasonable force by way of correction to maintain order and discipline in the classroom. In fact, this statutory authority has been and continues to be contained in the Criminal Code as a specific defence available to teachers against a charge of assaulting a student.

When we combine the growth of statutory authority with the historical evolution of the school setting, it is simply not realistic to suggest that in today's schools teachers may rely on the doctrine of in loco parentis. This has been confirmed by the Supreme Court of Canada in the 1984 case of Ogg-Moss v. The Queen.[3] This case involved an assault charge against a counsellor in a facility for mentally disabled adults. In his discussion of the application of section 43 of the Criminal Code, Chief Justice Dickson examined the history and application of in loco parentis. He concluded that the courts will be reluctant to imply a delegation of parental authority but would attempt to give effect to an express delegation.

Modern Day Roles of Teachers

Today's teachers face many complex and varying roles. Certainly, many teachers would welcome a return to the traditional in loco parentis model of teaching, when it was possible to simply rest on your judgment as a parent. In today's schools, the teacher is required to act not only as a parent but as a police officer, social worker, and professional educator. It is no wonder that many teachers feel confused and frustrated in their present circumstances and in particular with the conflicting signals sent to them by government officials, school administrators, and, more recently, the courts.

The chapters that follow identify and demystify these roles. In particular, they focus on the effect of the law on each of the modern teacher's roles. In many cases the law has served to create and enhance a particular role of teachers, and in other cases it has simply served to shift the boundaries of existing roles. It is fair to say that the law has become a source of confusion and frustration for teachers.

In preparing this book we have relied on our legal experience and research to a considerable extent. However, the primary basis for the particular definition of the roles of teachers was drawn from extensive seminars and lectures across the country — seminars where teachers have had the opportunity to voice their concerns and to ask questions. This interaction has allowed us to focus on the issues that cause the greatest concern among teachers. In a real way, teachers and administrators have assisted us in designing the structure of this book. For the purpose of analysis, we have divided this book into five chapters.

Chapter One deals with the "parental role" of teachers. While *in loco parentis* may no longer be a major doctrine for defining the legal status of teachers, its effects still linger in certain quasi-parental roles of teachers. This chapter includes a discussion of negligence and liability issues for teachers as well as a discussion of corporal punishment. It also examines the new sexual abuse provisions in the Criminal Code and points out the dangers to teachers inherent in these provisions.

Chapter Two deals with teachers as "educational state agents." The chapter includes a discussion of the duties of teachers as defined in the education statutes as well as the impact of the Charter and provincial human rights codes on teachers' actions in the classroom. This chapter includes a discussion of the right to an education, the validity of religious instruction in the schools, and other constitutionally entrenched rights enjoyed by both parents and students. We will also tackle the difficult area of making and enforcing school rules and touch on the issue of educational malpractice in Canada.

Chapter Three centres primarily on criminal law and the teacher as a state agent for the police. This involves an examination of the Young Offenders Act, the juvenile justice system in Canada, and the role played by teachers within that system. We look at various case law examples as well as at pressing issues such as search and seizure, detention, and the questioning of students.

Chapter Four deals with the teacher as social welfare agent. Increasingly, teachers are required to assume a social welfare responsibility for children. The most prominent example of this role is the requirement to report any suspected child abuse. The social welfare role has been expanded considerably in recent years. Guidance counsellors are now required to provide more assistance to students than mere advice on course selection. Teachers are often caught in the middle of family disputes and are required to act as mediators in cases where children are involved. Teachers may also be seen as resources for the various social agencies in the city. There is an increasing trend toward the involvement of teachers in "breakfast clubs" and clothing drives. It is not unusual for a teacher to become involved extensively with the parents, social workers, and group homes that affect the lives of particular students. The legal parameters of this new role are little understood.

Chapter Five explores the role of the teacher as an employee. Whereas the first four chapters deal primarily with teachers in relation to the needs of others, this chapter focuses on teachers' rights and obligations. The school is a complex workplace with myriad administrative structures and potential labour relations problems. Teachers are subject to strict collective bargaining procedures and various disciplinary proceedings. They may also experience lifestyle restrictions as part of their professional role. The chapter examines the labour and employment rights and duties of teachers. Teachers may be the beneficiaries as well as the targets of the new rights consciousness in society.

We hope that delineation of each of these roles will provide some answers to the troubling questions that face teachers every day. Teachers are the frontline contact with students, and are often required to make difficult decisions as situations arise in the classroom. By exploring the varied roles of teachers, we also hope to provide a framework for discussion. We are not attempting to answer all of the conceivable questions that may arise in the day-to-day operation of the classroom. However, by our providing a framework for discussion, there is a better chance that teachers, administrators, and provincial policy makers will share their experiences and create a more comfortable teaching environment — one with clearer expectations about what roles the teacher should play in the school.

In the chapters that follow it is important to keep in mind that our purpose is to identify and discuss some of these various roles rather than dissect them in a thorough legal fashion. This book is designed to be a practical reference guide for teachers — to assist them in their understanding of the complex legal issues that they face. We have not attempted to survey each issue thoroughly but have carefully researched the concepts that underlie each one. We have drawn upon the research and material that will form the basis of *Education Law in Canada* (2d edition),[4] and the reader is directed to that work for a thorough discussion of the issues raised in this book. It is our hope that this book will provide a useful framework for the exploration of important legal issues and help to demystify the law as it relates to teachers.

ENDNOTES

1. Pension (Teachers) Fund, R.S.B.C. 1979, c. 320 (as amended); Teachers' Retirement Fund Act, R.S.A. 1980, c. T-2 (as amended); Teaching Profession Act, R.S.A. 1980, c. T-3; School Buildings Act, R.S.A. 1980, c. S-4 (as amended); Teachers' Dental Plan Act, S.S. 1984-85-86, c. T-6.1 (as amended); Teachers Life Insurance (Government Contributory) Act, R.S.S. 1978, c. T-8 (as amended); Teachers' Pension Act, R.S.M. 1987, c. T20; Teachers' Society Act, R.S.M. 1987, c. T30; Teaching Profession Act, R.S.O. 1990, c. T.2; School Boards and Teachers Collective Negotiations Act, R.S.O. 1990, c. S.2; Teachers' Pension Act, R.S.N.B. 1973, c. T-1 (as amended); Teachers' Superannuation Act, R.S.P.E.I. 1988, c. T.1 (as amended); School Attendance (1978) Act, S.N. 1978, c. 78 (as amended); Newfoundland Teachers (Collective Bargaining) 1973 Act, S.N. 1973, c. 114 (as amended).

2. *Jowett's Dictionary of English Law*, 2d ed.

3. *Ogg-Moss v. The Queen* (1984), 11 D.L.R. (4th) 549 (S.C.C.).

4. Forthcoming in 1992 as an update of W. MacKay, *Education Law in Canada* (Toronto: Emond Montgomery, 1984).

1

Teachers as Parents

This chapter deals with those circumstances in the school setting that most often require a teacher to adopt a parental role with his or her students. In the introduction we discussed the limits of *in loco parentis* and its inapplicability to the modern school. Although *in loco parentis* may no longer define a teacher's legal status in the school, it has left its mark on the school environment and certainly on the hearts and minds of most teachers. This is most evident in the field of negligence.

Liability for Accidents at School

Negligence in the school setting is always of concern to teachers. Teachers frequently ask, "When can we be sued?" Before we can examine the principles of negligence in the school in any detail, it is important to set out the framework for the operation of negligence law. Cases that involve accidents at school fall into the common law category of "tort law." Torts may briefly be described as civil wrongs. The law of torts has been in a constant state of evolution since the early 1900s. The same tort principles that apply to society in general apply, with only slight modifications, to the school setting. There are two branches of tort law — negligence and intentional torts. We will turn first to negligence, which is the more significant branch.

Negligence Principles

Any court case that involves negligence will follow a basic four-step analysis:

(1) Was a duty of care owed to the injured person?
(2) What is the standard of care required by the situation?
(3) Was this standard of care breached?
(4) What damages, if any, were suffered by the injured person?

1

Regardless of the facts and the parties involved, a court will normally ask these four questions when it determines liability for negligence.

The term "negligence" is a familiar one. It is clearly negligent to drive on the wrong side of the road or to give a loaded gun to a two-year-old child. Both of these actions fall below the accepted standard of care owed to those around us and are likely to cause harm to others. A central concept of the law of negligence is that a person should be able to predict when his or her actions might create risks that could cause harm to others. Such risks should not be created. If risks must be taken, preventive measures should be adopted to diminish the chance of harm to others. This is the underlying philosophy of negligence, and it is the responsibility of the courts to hold parties accountable in cases where they have created risks or not taken reasonable measures to prevent risks of harm to others.

Duty of Care

When a court speaks of the "duty of care" to others, it is really saying that we all have a responsibility to take reasonable measures to avoid causing harm to others where the harm caused and the person injured are "reasonably foreseeable." We all know that when operating a car we must be careful to avoid causing accidents that involve other vehicles or pedestrians. Another vehicle on the road or a pedestrian crossing the street is "reasonably foreseeable" — that is, a reasonable person would expect to encounter other traffic and perhaps pedestrians while driving a car. With this in mind, a reasonable person drives in a way that will minimize the risk of accidents.

Some other examples of the duty of care are not quite as obvious. Should a tavern owner, for example, be responsible for injuries caused to a patron who has been served too many drinks? The Supreme Court of Canada has decided that it is reasonable in some circumstances to impose a duty of care on a tavern owner who allows a patron to become severely intoxicated and then leave the bar. In a case where a drunken patron left a tavern and was later struck by a car along the highway as he stumbled home, the court determined that it was appropriate to impose a duty of care on the owner of the bar.[1]

It is important to note that the imposition of a duty of care does not require a person to take steps to eliminate the possibility of harm, but only to take reasonable steps to minimize the risk of injury. Take the example of an outdoor hockey rink bordered by a pedestrian sidewalk: it is foreseeable that a pedestrian might be hit by a puck. The owner of the rink owes a duty to pedestrians to minimize the risk of injury from flying pucks. This duty probably does not require the owner to prohibit hockey games or completely enclose the rink. A reasonable person would probably erect boards and a screen; consequently, this would represent the standard of care the owner must meet.

Teachers and school authorities have special common law duties of care imposed on them because of the nature of their work. They are entrusted with the care of large numbers of young children, and this is a weighty responsibility. This duty exists inside and outside the classroom. The duty may begin before school hours and remain in effect after school hours. In short, teachers must take care in cases where students are involved to ensure that students are not exposed to any unnecessary risk of harm. When students are under the charge of teachers, a duty of care arises that can lead to legal liability.

Standard of Care

Although there is a consistent duty of care imposed on teachers, the standard of care will vary depending on the circumstances. Any number of factors can be involved in determining the appropriate standard of care. A court's primary task is to establish what a "reasonable person" would do in similar circumstances. It is difficult, therefore, to provide any precise guidelines by which a teacher may gauge his or her conduct. In essence, the question is one of good judgment. Teachers and school administrators can help each other by monitoring each other's conduct and having open discussions about appropriate conduct in given circumstances.

Many schools and school boards have policies or guidelines that provide teachers with some basis for determining whether their conduct is appropriate. These could include guidelines for the number of teachers required on playground supervision and defining the playground areas for which each teacher will be responsible. For physical education teachers, policies may restrict the number of children allowed to participate in dangerous activities (for example, archery) and require that "spotters" be assigned to all gymnastic equipment. One of the frequent complaints of principals is that some teachers are late in getting to their classrooms. If a child was injured while misbehaving prior to a teacher's arrival in the classroom, that teacher could be the subject of scrutiny by the courts.

It is in the area of standard of care that the ghost of in loco parentis haunts educators most prominently. The courts have determined that a teacher's standard of care is that of a "careful parent."[2] Teachers are expected to use the same degree of caution that careful or prudent parents would use in caring for their own children. Perhaps in a one-room school house with 10 or 15 students a teacher may be held to the standard of care of a careful or prudent parent. In today's schools, however, where teachers are often responsible for 30 or more students (or for hundreds on the playground), it is simply unrealistic for the courts to continue to impose the standard of care that would be exercised by parents over their own child.

This criticism of the careful parent rule has been raised frequently, both in and out of court, over the past number of decades. It has been targeted as a paternalistic and outmoded standard that places an extremely heavy burden on teachers. At the same time, the careful parent rule offers very little guidance for teachers in the assessment of their conduct and their attempts to avoid negligence. It also allows the courts to bend the standard in any way they desire, which makes it difficult for lawyers to predict the outcome of a negligence suit. In spite of these criticisms, the careful parent rule has been repeatedly upheld by the courts, and it is apparently a fact of life for teachers.

In spite of the uncertain standard set by the courts, the case law provides some examples of the factors that should be considered by teachers in determining appropriate conduct in a particular situation. A complete review of these cases is beyond the scope of this work; however, some of the following factors have been cited:

(1) the age of the student or students;
(2) the nature of the activity — is it inherently dangerous, or did the student do something unforeseeable to make the activity dangerous?
(3) the amount of instruction received by the student;
(4) the student's general awareness of the risks involved;
(5) the approved general practice and, in particular, any school policies regarding this practice;
(6) the foreseeable risk of danger; and
(7) previous accidents in similar circumstances.

There is no scientific method for determining the standard of care in any given situation. One of the best methods of ensuring that you are within the appropriate standard of care is to discuss potentially dangerous situations with colleagues. Often school accidents are precipitated by similar "near misses." Some creative staff room discussion about close calls may save everyone a lot of anguish down the road. Most important, these conversations may prevent a student from suffering a serious accident.

Breach of a Standard of Care

Once a court has set what it feels is the appropriate standard of care in the circumstances, it must determine whether the teacher has committed a breach of this standard. In other words, do the teacher's actions conform with the court's view of what the careful parent would have done in the circumstances? The law does not expect anyone to be perfect; it simply expects people to act reasonably. Teachers should simply act reasonably to minimize the occurrence of accidents.

The courts must also consider whether the student has contributed to his or her own misfortune. This will rarely apply to very young children, who should be subjected to more restrictive supervision. However, a teenage student may be found to be "contributorily negligent," thereby reducing the teacher's liability. Most provinces have statutes that deal with contributory negligence and allow the courts to apportion the amount of liability that should be attached to each party.[3]

The issue of contributory negligence illustrates a dynamic tension that pervades all aspects of a teacher's duties, and particularly a teacher's responsibility for negligence. On the one hand, a teacher must supervise and protect the students within his or her charge; this demands a certain degree of paternalism. On the other hand, one of the teacher's most important educational goals is to produce independent and self-reliant children who are capable of looking after themselves. In this respect, the teacher faces the same dilemma as the parent: How do you protect a child from the many risks of the outside world without smothering his or her inherent spirit of adventure and need for independence? This issue was addressed by an English judge who refused to find a teacher negligent for leaving handicraft knives easily accessible. The presence of these knives later resulted in injuries from student horseplay. The judge stated: "It is better that a boy should break his neck than allow other people to break his spirit."[4]

This quotation is admittedly a drastic statement, but the principle is well taken. It does provide a stark illustration of the teacher's need to strike a balance between adequately protecting students and giving them enough freedom to develop their independence. Teachers must walk a fine line.

Damages

The fourth necessary element of a tort is that the plaintiff must have suffered some ascertainable damage, as recognized by law. In most cases money is paid as compensation for damages suffered as a result of an injury. This is not always the case, however. The law also makes provision for other remedies such as injunctions, which involve a court order that directs the parties to maintain or discontinue a certain course of action. We will discuss the importance and availability of injunctions as Charter remedies later on in this book; injunctions rarely arise in school negligence cases. A school board may certainly alter its policies or conduct as a result of losing a case in negligence (for example, by implementing more detailed safety procedures); however, the court rarely orders a board to do so.

The principle that damages must be sustained before an action can be successful is similar to the common sense notion of "no harm, no foul." The harm, however, does not necessarily mean actual physical harm; it can take the form of nervous shock or emotional distress provided that there is some substantial evidence of these conditions. Aside from the judicial requirement of damages, there is a practical economic component to this principle. Litigation is a very expensive process and there is no point in pursuing a court action in cases where the recovery would be so minimal that the legal fees would not be covered. Even if a party is successful in litigation and is awarded costs by the court, these court-ordered costs rarely compensate the plaintiff for more than one-third of the actual legal costs. Thus the damages claim must be large enough to make the litigation worthwhile.

The practical necessity for substantial damages in a school negligence case should reduce the fear of being sued where the damage to a child is minimal. For instance, if you are not paying proper attention on the playground and a child engages in a dangerous activity but simply skins his or her knee, there is no need to be overly concerned about a lawsuit. There may be some in-school repercussions through disciplinary procedures, but court action is highly unlikely.

There may, however, be severe damage caused to a child through accidents in the most innocuous situations. At a recent seminar, one teacher discussed a situation where a five-year-old child had severely cut his arm while sliding down a large slide head first on the playground. The ground at the foot of the slide was gravel and rocks. The cut had not been severe enough to instigate any legal action; however, the possibility of a severe head or neck injury from the same scenario is staggering. These are exactly the kinds of situations in which teachers must be aware. This is certainly a case where an ounce of prevention is worth a pound of cure.

Vicarious Liability

Cases that involve the negligence of teachers, principals, or other school employees will usually result in a finding of liability against the relevant school board under the doctrine of "vicarious liability."

If a teacher or other employee of the school board is negligent, he or she is personally liable in damages but the employing school board, which is normally in a better position to compensate the victim, is often the primary defendant. The school board as employer is normally found liable for the acts of its employees.

The doctrine of vicarious liability originates in the law of master and servant; initially, the employer was only liable for acts that resulted from the employer's order. Vicarious liability has now been expanded to all torts committed by an employee while acting in the course of employment and extends well beyond actions that were expressly mandated by the employer. The rationale behind expanding the doctrine of vicarious liability is to provide a more reasonable allocation of the loss. It is the school board and not the teacher who can afford to compensate victims of negligence and the school board is consequently in a better position to carry insurance for these accidents. School boards also have an economic incentive to prevent accidents and to discipline their employees for unreasonable conduct.

The concept of "course of employment" is elusive. In recent times, most actions of employees have been held to be in the course of employment. Even actions that have been expressly forbidden by the employer have been held by the courts to be in the course of employment. In fact, the Supreme Court of Canada has relied on the doctrine of vicarious liability to find that an employer may be liable for the actions of an employee that result in sexual harassment.[5] This may be used as a bench mark to show the broad scope of the phrase "course of employment."

If the employee is on a "frolic of his own" and is, in effect, acting as a stranger in respect to his or her employer, no liability attaches to the employer. Actions that are a means of carrying out the job — albeit negligently or even in breach of express rules — are still in the "course of employment." The following may provide a useful formulation of the test:

> The test is whether a wrongful act is a mode of performing the general duties of the servant's employment: whether the servant was about his master's business at the time.[6]

One example of a case in which the actions of a teacher were held to be outside the scope of her employment is *Beauparlent v. Board of Trustees of Separate School Section No. 1 of Appleby*.[7] In this case, teachers in the school decided to transport nearly 70 students to a concert in a nearby town. The concert was being held in honour of a priest's birthday; the court concluded that the activity was not connected to the course of studies. Transportation for the outing was a stakebody truck that was provided by a citizen in the community and that had not been inspected for safety. On the way into town, chains on the back of the truck broke and several children were thrown onto the highway; severe injuries resulted. No board permission had been obtained for the trip and the school board was found not liable for the accident because the teachers were acting outside the scope of their authority.

It is indeed difficult to find many examples where the courts have refused to find a school board vicariously liable for the actions of teachers. The obvious economic reality is that the courts are tempted by the "deep pockets" of the school board's insurance company, and averse to potentially bankrupting an individual teacher. Particularly with children, serious permanent injuries (short of death) result in potentially large damage awards. Where there is a significant cost of future care, the courts may certainly be inclined to hold the board liable so that the child may have access to the resources of the board's insurance policy. It is important that the injured student not be denied proper compensation.

A spontaneous class outing to a local restaurant in the teacher's car could expose him or her to personal liability. It is advisable to seek approval for such trips either from the principal or, preferably, from the school board itself. Teachers who have occasion to transport students in their own vehicle, for any reason, should check with their insurance company to ensure that they have adequate personal coverage. The potential financial risk of such transportation may not be not covered in a standard insurance policy.

Activities directly related to the course of studies are much more likely to be found within the course of employment. The school board was held vicariously liable in a case where a 14-year-old student was instructed to poke the fire in a school room so that a teacher could have a hot lunch.[8] The student's pinafore caught fire and she was injured. Fortunately, we no longer have open fires or pinafores in today's classrooms. The point, however, is that the courts have historically taken a broad approach to defining the scope of a teacher's employment and school boards will usually be found liable for the acts of their employees.[9]

Insurance

As mentioned earlier, one of the primary purposes for expanding the doctrine of vicarious liability is to allocate losses in a reasonable manner. It is obvious that school boards are in a much better economic position to obtain adequate insurance to cover the losses suffered across their school network. This is more economically efficient than individual teachers or administrators taking out independent insurance policies. The teacher is, therefore, reasonably protected from the financial repercussions of their conduct in the schools. Of course, if a teacher's negligence shows a complete disregard for his or her responsibilities or particularly bad judgment, he or she may be subject to discipline and possibly dismissal.

From the above discussion of insurance and vicarious liability, it is obvious that teachers are well protected in the area of negligence. However, from a practical point of view, you should always remember that litigation is a very uncomfortable process in which you are the object of the court's scrutiny. The teacher, even if not financially responsible for the case, will still be a defendant in the litigation and thus subject to the trial and discovery processes. Where an accident has resulted in severe injuries to a child, it is terribly disturbing to be continually forced to relive the incident under the scrutiny of lawyers and judges. To protect the students from harm and themselves from litigation, all teachers should be on the lookout for potentially dangerous situations.

Application of Negligence in the School

Having set up the general framework for a discussion of negligence liability in the schools, we now turn to a review of some of the specific opportunities in a school for accidents to arise. As we indicated, negligence cases are very fact-specific.

The Classroom

Teachers are rarely sued for their actions or inactions while in the classroom, although that is where they spend most of their time. Most accidents occur in the hallways or playgrounds, or on field trips. The major exceptions to this generalization are physical education teachers and shop teachers, who do attract lawsuits while performing the main task for which they are employed. Their liability is discussed later in this chapter.

A teacher has the duty to supervise the students while in the classroom but, as mentioned earlier, it is when the teacher is absent from the classroom that accidents are more likely to occur. There is surprisingly little case law in Canada with regard to classroom accidents; however, there are a couple of U.S. cases that provide some guidance. In one case, a teacher left her special education class unattended for about five minutes and instructed a neighbouring teacher to supervise the class.[10] One of her students was injured by another in a scuffle. The neighbouring teacher heard only the usual noise of a play period in the adjoining room. The U.S. court took note of the fact that the teacher was only absent for a few minutes and found no liability on the part of the teacher.

In another U.S. case,[11] a grade 4 student was accidentally injured by another student when the teacher left the room during calisthenics. The exercises were conducted by the children following a recording. The court stated that the injury was not a reasonably foreseeable result of the teacher's absence and was not caused by the absence of the teacher but rather by the other student. The court concluded that the accident would have occurred whether or not the teacher was there. Thus, even if the teacher were negligent, there was no causal connection between the relevant acts and the injury.

These cases should not be read as justifying absence from the classroom. The reasons for the absence, its duration, the type of accident, and the nature of the class are all factors that could lead to a finding of negligence in a Canadian court. The above scenario where a teacher is five minutes late getting to class but has not provided any instructions for supervision could, for example, easily set up a potential liability situation. One example of a classroom situation that could result in teacher liability is noon-hour supervision. Students often tend to become unruly during lunch, when school rules are much less clearly defined. This is particularly important to teachers in Manitoba where noon-hour supervision has been held to be a necessarily incidental part of their collective agreement.[12]

Playgrounds and Outside

When a child is injured outside a school, the question arises whether an adequate system of supervision was in place and, if it was, whether the teachers responsible for supervision adequately performed their tasks. If the inadequacy of the system was the cause of the accident, the principal or other person responsible for supervision of school premises will be liable. In a recent Ontario case, for example, a school board was sued when a student was cut on the back of his head with a snowball after school hours.[13] The incident occurred sometime between 3:30 p.m. (the time of dismissal of students) and 3:45 p.m. and there was no teacher supervising the playground at that time. It was the policy of the school for students to leave the school building and schoolgrounds immediately upon dismissal. Students riding buses were kept in the main lobby of the school until they were ready to board. The action was brought against the school board for not having an adequate system of supervision after school hours, not against a particular teacher. The

Ontario court dismissed the case and held that the school board's policy of not having teacher supervision was reasonable.

There have also been circumstances in which the system of supervision set up by the school board was found to be inadequate by the courts and liability attached. In *Tommy George v. Board of School Trustees, School District 70 (Port Alberni)*,[14] a five-year-old boy was injured when he was struck by a school bus being parked at the schoolgrounds to load passengers. In this case, the kindergarten was housed in a portable unit, separate from the main school building. It was not hooked up with the main P.A. system or bell system. In the rest of the school, there was a bell and a P.A. announcement that let the children know when they could leave the classroom for the school buses. The principal would wait until the school buses were all in place before making the announcement. The teacher in this case was held not to be negligent because she was responsible for 15 or 16 young children and could not be expected to get them all out of the classroom and also keep them all under supervision until they were on the parking lot. In the court's view, she was following a normal routine and had no reason to suspect that there was any unusual danger. The bus driver was held 40 percent negligent for not properly checking his mirrors and the school board was held 60 percent liable for having an inadequate system of communication in the school.

Of course, a teacher will be liable if his or her failure to provide proper supervision results in an injury to a student. The Supreme Court of Canada in *Board of Education for the City of Toronto v. Higgs*[15] held that there was no liability in a case where a bully injured another student. The court was not satisfied that increased supervision would have prevented the injury. The court did indicate that the known mischievous tendencies of the bully increased the range of foreseeable risks. There was no discussion by the court about whether teachers have a duty to inform themselves about the various tendencies of the children on the playground. Certainly, the effect of having more information available to the teacher would expand the range of foreseeable risks and thus liability.

A teacher will not be liable for inadequate supervision on the school grounds unless it can be shown that he or she should have seen the incident in sufficient time to prevent the injury. Therefore, when, out of several hundred students, a small group of boys was tossing acorns, there was no liability on the four supervising teachers for failing to see and stop this conduct before one of the boys was hit in the eye.[16] The principal made it a practice after that case to announce on the first day of school his rule against throwing any objects on the school grounds. Such a practice makes it easy to verify the exact date of the announcement if the need arises later in court.

Perhaps the safest course is to distribute a written statement of school rules to teachers, parents, and students; there are some other compelling reasons for distributing school rules and these will be discussed later in this book.

Before School Begins

Where students habitually arrive at school early, those who have the duty to provide supervision of school grounds may have to ensure that this supervision is in place. The responsible person is usually the principal or other administrator rather than an individual teacher. When a student was injured before school by a paperclip shot from an elastic band, the principal was said to have been negligent in failing to provide an adequate system of supervision and in failing to set rules for the students.[17] The court noted that because the students were expected to arrive early, the principal's responsibility arose before classes began. Parents should not, however, be unilaterally able to add to the duties of the school by dropping their children off at school early in the day.[18]

A duty may arise even though the school board regulations do not expressly require preschool supervision because, once the students are at school, they are beyond parental protection and control. In addition, by permitting the students to arrive early, the teacher-student relationship is created and the associated responsibilities are assumed by the teacher. These conclusions were reached by an Australian court in *Geyer v. Downs*,[19] where an eight-year-old student was injured when playing, unsupervised, on the school grounds before school. Although a teacher will rarely be responsible for providing a system of supervision, a teacher may be liable if he or she is assigned to supervise and is negligent. The major responsibility for preschool supervision appears to rest with the principal of the school.

It is advisable to establish clear hours of supervision both before and after school and to communicate these hours to the parents. If a child consistently appears at school early, the matter should be raised with the parents. While teachers should not be expected to act as preschool babysitters, school administrators should be clear about when supervision will and will not be offered and there must be some flexibility.

After School Ends

Similar problems of responsibility for supervision arise at the end of the day. What responsibility, if any, does a school official have once the child leaves the school? In most cases, it is reasonable to assume that children will be able to make it home safely from school, although this may not be true if the children are quite young. The foreseeability of harm is increased if the teacher ignores the parents' express instructions about the child's departure.

In recent years, the issue of the transfer of custody from the school to the parent has become more complex. Where buses are involved, it is a school board responsibility. In a city school where children walk home, there may be a greater responsibility on the teacher. A working parent may require that the child go to a daycare centre on certain days and to the child's home on others. Such instructions may be difficult for a young child to follow and the teacher may be expected to give some guidance. In any event, the ultimate responsibility rests with the parent to ensure that a reasonable system is in place. A teacher should not be expected to phone to make sure a parent is home before sending a child home for lunch, but if the child specifically expresses doubt, there may be a duty to inquire. Similarly, a teacher should not be expected to babysit students for long periods after school; however, emergencies, such as snow storms, can extend the time during which school authorities are responsible for students.

In *Barnes v. Hampshire County Council*,[20] five-year-old children who were always met by parents at an appointed time were released early. A child whose parent had not arrived yet wandered onto a nearby highway and was struck by a car. The court held that the early release created a risk that some children might not be met by parents and would try to make their own way home. It was foreseeable that a child might be injured trying to do that and the school authorities were consequently held negligent. The fact that the release was only five minutes early did not matter, because exact timing was crucial to the particular system upon which parents and school authorities had agreed.

Vocational (Shop) Classes and Science Labs

When dealing with accidents in cooking, woodworking, or auto repair classes, common sense dictates a greater degree of supervision. Thus, where a classroom had gas stoves with open flames, the school authorities were found negligent in not supplying a guard to prevent students from being burned, because this could have been reasonably anticipated. By analogy, a school would be expected to provide proper protection and give adequate warnings in the use of all forms of equipment in home economics and shop classes.

The general test to follow in any vocational class situation is to ensure that proper instructions are given for all of the equipment in addition to maintaining proper supervision throughout the class. In one case, a student was "flicking" a chisel near a sanding wheel and as a result the chisel hit the wheel and was driven into his leg. The court decided that the machine was not inherently dangerous, that sufficient supervision was maintained, and that the student was solely responsible for his injury.[21] In a more recent British Columbia case,[22] a 16-year-old grade 11 student was injured while moving sheets of plywood during his woodworking class. The sheets of plywood were stored in an unused boys' washroom across the hall from the actual woodworking class. The student required a three-quarter inch mahogany plywood sheet to finish a project on which he was working. The shop teacher escorted the student across the hall and explained how the student could safely remove the sheet of plywood from the storage area. He told the student specifically to get help from another student when moving the plywood. The student ignored these instructions and his left knee was crushed when the sheets of plywood fell on top of him.

The court accepted the teacher's testimony with regard to the instructions given to the student. The school board's lawyers had led evidence to establish the teacher's general practice and habits in instructing students on safety precautions. The court found the teacher to be conscientious and held that the instructions given in this particular instance were sufficient to meet the standard of care. The lesson to be learned from this case is that all vocational teachers should establish routine safety procedures and perhaps written safety manuals with adequate instructions so that, if there is any question about particular instructions given in a case where a student is injured, the court will have evidence of the good safety habits of the individual teacher.

The age and ability of the students in any class, but particularly a vocational class, can add to the standard of care that a teacher is expected to meet. If the students suffer from physical or mental disabilities, the range of foreseeable risks is likely to increase. This would be true not only for a class of disabled students but also for a single disabled child who has been integrated into a regular classroom setting. In *Dziwenka v. The Queen*,[23] the Supreme Court of Canada held a woodworking teacher to a higher standard of care when a deaf student was injured on a power saw. The student's lack of hearing put him at greater risk around power tools and the teacher had a higher standard of care in respect to this child, who became the victim of an injury.

When dealing with a science experiment that may pose a potential danger to students, a teacher should ensure that appropriate safety precautions are explained and safety equipment provided. In *James v. River East School Division No. 9*,[24] a student was injured when chemicals splattered in her face. She was not wearing safety glasses, and the procedure for the chemistry experiment required her to look into the vessel to determine the progress of the chemical reaction. The teacher was held liable for failing to instruct the students adequately with respect to the potential hazards and, in particular, with respect to the possibility of splattering. The court also held that the procedure itself was negligent because it required the student to look into the vessel. It is important to note that the procedure was followed in the past without incident; however, this did not afford an excuse. Although past practice may be used as a defence against a claim of negligence, if the practice itself is found to be negligent, it provides no defence. A practice does not cease to be negligent just because it is frequently repeated.

Although most teachers would assume that woodworking classes and science labs are inherently the most dangerous, the possibility of accidents in other classrooms must always be taken into account. In a recent case in Ontario, a male grade 8 student suffered an eye injury as a result of an accident with a sewing machine in a family studies class.[25] The students, including the boy who suffered the injury, were given an assignment to sew a piece of broadcloth. The students had no prior sewing experience. The teacher instructed the students to stop the machines if they had a problem and to come to her for assistance. The injured boy experienced "bunching" or "sewing on the spot." The teacher had not instructed the class specifically about bunching and had not instructed the class to stop sewing when bunching occurred. As a result of the bunching, the needle in the sewing machine shattered and caused a permanent injury to the student's right cornea.

The court held that it was reasonably foreseeable that a needle could break from sewing on the spot and that it could shatter and strike a user in the eye, even though this was admittedly an unusual occurrence. The court confirmed that the standard of care to be exercised by the teacher in providing supervision was that of a careful or prudent parent. In these circumstances, the court held the teacher (and the school board vicariously) liable for not providing adequate instruction. The teacher was dealing with first-year sewers. A reasonably intelligent student experiencing bunching for the first time would not automatically recognize the problem and call for the teacher's assistance. The court held that the teacher should have been more precise in her safety instructions. The court also concluded that the student did not act completely reasonably in the circumstances and found the student to be 10 percent contributorily negligent.

Sports

Injuries are most likely to occur in school sports activities, although most will not give rise to school liability. Accidents do occur even when no one has been negligent, and a school cannot be an ensurer of the safety of all students under its care. There is an inherent risk of injury in most athletic activities, and only if the student is exposed to unreasonable risks will the teacher be considered negligent.[26] Because of the strenuous activities carried on in the gymnasium, the injuries that result from accidents are often very serious and the chance of getting a substantial damages award in the courts is greater.[27] This may explain the relatively large number of physical education-related cases brought before the courts.

Traditionally, the test to be applied in determining whether a physical education teacher was negligent is that of the careful parent. This was the conclusion reached in *McKay v. Board of Govan School Unit No. 29*,[28] where the school was found liable for injuries to a student who was performing on the parallel bars. The student's lack of experience in the relevant manoeuvres was a critical factor. The traditional standard has been reaffirmed in recent Supreme Court of Canada decisions such as *Myers v. Peel County Board of Education*.[29]

In the light of the specialized training of the instructors and the complexity of athletic activity, the careful parent standard may no longer be appropriate for physical education instructors. In *Thornton v. Board of School Trustees of School District No. 57*,[30] a decision of the Supreme Court of Canada, a 15-year-old student became a quadriplegic as a result of doing a somersault from a springboard. The physical education teacher was found negligent for not realizing that the addition of a box for jumping created a dangerous situation. He also had failed to stop the exercise to determine the cause of a similar accident in which a student broke his wrist. The teacher had been working on school reports rather than supervising the several athletic activities that were taking place in the gymnasium. In spite of the high damages award against the school board, the teacher continued to teach in the same school system.

Both the trial judge in *Thornton*[31] and the B.C. Court of Appeal[32] had held that the teacher had a duty to meet the standard of care of a reasonably skilled physical education instructor rather than that of a careful parent. The Supreme Court of Canada was not required to address that issue on appeal; that court concluded that the teacher was negligent by either standard.

At the appeal level, the B.C. court stated a four-point test that has been cited in most subsequent cases. There will be no negligence on the part of the physical education instructor who permits a student to engage in gymnastics, such as a somersault off a spring board,

(1) if the exercise is suitable to his age and condition (mental and physical);
(2) if he is progressively trained and coached to do it properly and avoid the danger;
(3) if the equipment is adequate and suitably arranged; and
(4) if the performance, having regard to its inherently dangerous nature, is properly supervised.[33]

In *Myers et al. v. Peel County Board of Education et al.*,[34] a 15-year-old boy was severely injured while attempting a dismount from suspended rings. At the trial,[35] the judge applied the higher standard of the reasonably competent physical education teacher used by the Court of Appeal in *Thornton*; but the Ontario Court of Appeal[36] and the Supreme Court of Canada reaffirmed the careful parent standard as the appropriate one.

In applying the careful parent test, the Supreme Court said that this standard will vary depending on the number of students, the nature of the activity, the student's age, the degree of skill and training, the nature and condition of the equipment used, the competency and capacity of the students, and "a host of other matters."[37] By taking all these factors into account in determining the careful parent standard, the court suggests that a physical education teacher may be held to a higher standard because of his or her more detailed knowledge of the condition and capacity of the students and the nature of the activity and equipment used.

Emergencies

Physical education teachers are the ones most frequently confronted with emergency situations. However, emergencies can happen to regular classroom teachers as well. The supervising teacher on a field trip may be directly confronted with an emergency situation. A dramatic illustration of this is provided by *Moddejonge v. Huron County Board of Education*[38] in which two young girls drowned. The teacher, who was the coordinator of the outdoor education program, was unable to swim. During an outing, he took five girls (at their request) to a nearby swimming spot for a brief swim. The teacher pointed out that there was a dangerous dropoff in the lake and he warned them to stay away from it. However, a breeze carried two of the girls out to the dropoff point where they encountered trouble. One of these girls was a non-swimmer. A third girl came to the rescue and saved one of the girls but was herself drowned along with the other girl she attempted to rescue. The defendant teacher who could not swim had to return to camp to seek assistance from another supervising teacher. On these facts, it was not difficult for the court to conclude that the teacher's conduct fell below that of the careful parent. What is surprising is that the teacher was held to be acting in the course of his employment and the school board was found to be vicariously liable.

If the teacher is the person providing emergency aid, he or she must perform competently. This underscores the need for teachers who are in charge of field trips or high-risk in-school activities to be trained to cope with emergencies. A basic understanding of first aid and life-saving techniques, such as C.P.R., is a minimum but there is often no such school requirement. The elimination of all outings may be a safe legal response but it is not a good educational one. Fear of legal liability should not prevent teachers from challenging their students in creative ways.

Emergency situations may necessitate medical action either at the hands of a supervising teacher or on his or her authorization. Acquiring parental consent may be impractical, if not impossible. Most provincial hospital acts or the regulations made under them permit medical treatment without proper consent in order to save life, limb, or vital organ. There is a legal presumption that a child consents to life-saving procedures. If the parent objects to such procedures (for example, a Jehovah's Witness who does not believe in blood transfusions), special problems arise; however, a thorough discussion of these issues is beyond the scope of this book. Whenever possible, it is advisable to get medical consents before embarking on a field trip.

The Criminal Code also has a role to play in the issue of emergency medical treatment. Sections 216 and 217 prohibit a teacher whether acting as a rescuer or not from undertaking acts dangerous to life. There is a defence of necessity under section 8(3) of the Code, however, that might be relied upon. There is the further possibility of a charge of criminal negligence under sections 219, 220, and 221 of the Criminal Code. This possibility arises in cases where a teacher's negligence is so extreme as to show a "wanton or reckless disregard for the lives or safety of other persons." Criminal charges may arise where death or serious bodily harm results from the negligence, but most cases are pursued in the civil rather than criminal arena. Charges of criminal negligence against teachers are very rare in Canada.

If a teacher takes reasonable measures to cope with an emergency, a successful lawsuit against him or her is unlikely. It is also wise for teachers who may be exposed to potentially dangerous situations to have some proper training in emergency procedures. Remember that the standard expected is not that of perfection but rather that of the careful parent.[39]

Liability for Corporal Punishment in Schools

In legal terms, any touching without consent is a technical assault. In real terms, legal action is only likely where the touching results in some physical or emotional damage to the victim. An assault can lead to both a civil action for the intentional torts of assault and battery and a claim in negligence. There is also a criminal sanction for an assault against a person. Thus a teacher can face legal action in both civil and criminal courts without being in a legal situation of double jeopardy. With respect to children, there is a Criminal Code defence (under section 43) to what might otherwise be categorized as an assault and this same kind of defence has been considered in civil actions as well. It is possible that this adverse treatment of the young may violate the Charter guarantees of equality and that section 43 of the Criminal Code may be unconstitutional age discrimination under section 15 of the Charter, but this issue has not yet arisen in the courts. We will proceed to explain the current state of the laws.

The issue of corporal punishment in the school is perhaps one of the most stark examples of the parental role of teachers, particularly as derived from the old notion of *in loco parentis*. The issue of corporal punishment in schools has largely been laid to rest by school board policies that prohibit its use. Only Newfoundland, British Columbia, and the Yukon expressly deal with the issue of corporal punishment in their statutes and regulations. It is still permitted under the Newfoundland and Yukon statutes, and is specifically prohibited in British Columbia. However, the Criminal Code protections for teachers to use force by way of correction remain in existence in the form of section 43:

> Every schoolteacher, parent or person standing in the place of a parent is justified in using force by way of correction toward a pupil or child, as the case may be, who is under his care, if the force does not exceed what is reasonable under the circumstances.

One of the most striking features of this section of the Criminal Code is that it identifies school teachers separately from "persons standing in the place of a parent." If teachers truly stood *in loco parentis*, there would be no need to separately identify them as a category in section

43 of the Criminal Code. This section provides further evidence of the demise of the *in loco parentis* doctrine as an operative source of authority for teachers.

Although corporal punishment may no longer form the basis of day-to-day correction in the school setting, there are recent cases where the courts have been called upon to review a teacher's disciplinary actions in the criminal law context. In *R. v. Dimmel*,[40] a teacher was acquitted of an assault charge in a case where he had "shaken some sense" into a student who was being openly defiant. Similarly, in a more recent British Columbia case,[41] a 17-year-old student, while entering the school one morning, yelled across the school grounds at the teacher a number of times calling him "Papa Smurf." The teacher responded by slapping the student on the side of the head. The trial judge stated that the words used and the manner in which they were said were defiant and rude. He found that section 43 of the Criminal Code applied and justified the use of this force by way of correction, as reasonable in the circumstances. The age and size of the student were factors considered by the judge in reaching his conclusion.

In spite of these judicial affirmations of section 43, it is not a recommended practice for teachers to resort to physical violence as a means of correction. Perhaps a more practical example of the application of section 43 is provided in *R. v. Sweet*.[42] In this case, three teachers had reason to believe that three students, including the accused, had been smoking marijuana in one of the classrooms. They asked the three students to stand against the wall and wait for the vice-principal who was called to deal with the incident. Two students complied with the request while the accused refused. The teachers refused to let the student leave and the student tried to push his way past one of the teachers to proceed down the hallway. The student was stopped by one teacher and, in an attempt to escape, the student elbowed the teacher in the mid-section and bit his left hand.

The student was charged with assault and, at the trial, alleged that he was justified in using the force necessary to avoid detention because the detention was unlawful under the Charter of Rights. The judge dismissed the Charter arguments and in the course of his reasoning said that the actions of the teachers in attempting to use force to keep the student in place were reasonable, regardless of whether the student had actually been smoking marijuana. The judge also said that section 43 permits force by teachers where there is a reasonable and probable, although mistaken, belief that the student has committed a breach of discipline.

In *R. v. Haberstock*,[43] a teacher slapped the face of a student who, he thought, had called him names from the window of a departing school bus. The punishment was administered on Monday morning for a Friday afternoon incident. Even though it was admitted that the teacher had punished the wrong student, the Saskatchewan Court of Appeal dismissed the charge because it was a reasonable mistake for the teacher to make. The trial court had found the teacher guilty of assault on the basis that punishment for an activity that the student did not engage in could not be regarded as "for correction." It appears that teachers have, for better or worse, been well protected by the courts in these cases.

In addition to the criminal cases, it should also be remembered that any discipline by way of physical force opens up potential liability issues in negligence or the intentional tort of assault. If the discipline is handed out incorrectly, there is a potential for a civil action by the student. If, for example, in the *Sweet* case the teacher had attempted incorrectly to restrain the student by using a judo manoeuvre and had broken an arm or a leg, there would be potential civil liability. Of course, such use of force may be necessary in some circumstances and the teacher has a right to defend himself or herself.

There has been considerable lobbying by many groups over the past number of years to eliminate the protections provided by section 43 of the Code. The courts have not yet had the occasion to test section 43 of the Criminal Code against section 12 of the Charter, which protects everyone from cruel and unusual punishment or treatment, or the protections of fundamental justice in section 7 of the Charter. Given the rare use of corporal punishment in today's schools, it may be that the courts will not be given that opportunity. Although some forms of particularly humiliating discipline may be found to violate the Charter protections against cruel and unusual treatment, it is unlikely that simple corporal punishment issues would invoke Charter protections. As mentioned earlier, section 43 may also be subject to an equality challenge under section 15 of the Charter. At present, many would prefer to have section 43 remain a part of the Criminal Code and allow the teaching profession and school boards to police themselves. The fact that a court may uphold certain physical forms of discipline as not "criminal" behaviour does not preclude a school board from finding it inappropriate and taking disciplinary action. With respect to the issue of corporal punishment, educators have been more progressive than judges in restricting or eliminating this form of discipline. The commonly held view by teachers that the law does not allow one to use force to discipline a student is not supported in the case law. It is school policies, responding to public opinion, that have limited the use of force by teachers.

Sexual Interference and Invitation to Sexual Touching: The Teacher's Liability

In today's schools, perhaps one of the most dangerous aspects of the "parental role" of teachers involves the new Criminal Code provisions on sexual interference and invitation to sexual touching. Teachers, particularly male teachers in elementary school settings, who think of themselves as standing in the place of the parent, can be in for a severe shock when they run up against criminal law. The changes to criminal law now make it an offence (punishable by imprisonment for up to 10 years) to touch, directly or indirectly, any part of the body of a young person for a sexual purpose. The sections of the Code are reproduced below:

151. Every person who, for a sexual purpose, touches, directly or indirectly, with a part of the body or with an object, any part of the body of a person under the age of fourteen years is guilty of an indictable offence and liable to imprisonment for a term not exceeding ten years or is guilty of an offence punishable on summary conviction.

152. Every person who, for a sexual purpose, invites, counsels or incites a person under the age of fourteen years to touch, directly or indirectly, with a part of the body or with an object, the body of any person, including the body of the person who so invites, counsels or incites and the body of the person under the age of fourteen years, is guilty of an indictable offence and liable to imprisonment for a term not exceeding ten years or is guilty of an offence punishable on summary conviction.

153.(1) Every person who is in a position of trust or authority towards a young person or is a person with whom the young person is in a relationship of dependency and who

(a) for a sexual purpose, touches, directly or indirectly, with a part of the body or with an object, any part of the body of the young person, or

(b) for a sexual purpose, invites, counsels or incites a young person to touch, directly or indirectly, with a part of the body or with an object, the body of any person, including the body of the person who so invites, counsels or incites and the body of the young person,

is guilty of an indictable offence and liable to imprisonment for a term not exceeding five years or is guilty of an offence punishable on summary conviction.

(2) In this section, "young person" means a person fourteen years of age or more but under the age of eighteen years.

For any criminal offence, the proof of the offence in court is broken into two elements: the *actus reus* and the *mens rea*. The first requires the Crown to prove the actual act complained of and the second requires the Crown to prove the intent of the accused to commit the offence. Whenever the police are informed of the *actus reus* of an offence, they are entitled to commence an investigation to determine whether there is any evidence of the necessary mental element to establish the offence. For instance, in a murder case, the act of stabbing someone is reducible to manslaughter if you cannot prove that the person intended to kill the victim.

In the case of sexual interference, every time a teacher touches a young child, he or she has, on a strict reading of the Criminal Code, committed the *actus reus* of a criminal offence and may be subject to investigation and possible prosecution. The job for the police and the Crown prosecutor is to show that the touching was done for a "sexual purpose." This is a substantial task and there must be proof "beyond a reasonable doubt" of the sexual intent, before a conviction can be entered. However, all teachers are painfully aware that the fact of a conviction is quite minor compared with the devastating effect of the allegations becoming public through an investigation in the community.

Legislators have further made life difficult for teachers by amending evidentiary sections of the Code, which now provide that a conviction may be obtained on the testimony of a child alone, without corroborating evidence — that is, the testimony of another witness to back up the child's story. Before this amendment, it was necessary to have some other objective physical evidence of the assault before the court could rely on the testimony of a child. There is also no presumption that a recent complaint is more valid than a complaint made months or years after an incident allegedly occurred. The revised section 715.1 of the Code also allows video-taped evidence, in which the complainant describes the acts complained of, to be admitted into court without requiring the child to go through the events on the witness stand. The precise situations in which such tapes can be used and the purposes of such evidence are still being worked out in court decisions. The Crown is now in the habit of having social workers interview the child with a video camera to preserve the child's evidence.

These provisions may seem excessively harsh and terribly drastic in their implications for teachers; however, the problems of child abuse in our society are such that Parliament felt it necessary to take these measures. One illustration of the previous inadequacy of the Criminal Code is illustrated by a case involving a teacher in British Columbia — *R. v. Cadden*.[44] In this case, a teacher was charged with sexual assault against five young boys (aged 9 and 10), where the evidence was that he invited boys during class to crawl under his desk in the classroom and perform various sexual acts on him. There was no actual touching by the teacher of the children. He simply gave verbal instructions of what he wanted them to do. The case went to the B.C. Court of Appeal because the defence argued there could be no sexual assault without actual touching by the complainant. Words alone do not constitute an assault. The B.C. Court of Appeal held that the combination of words and gestures used by the teacher constituted a threat to invade the bodily integrity of the victims and, therefore, constituted an assault within the meaning of the Criminal Code. There is no question that the court had to stretch the meaning of the Criminal Code in order to obtain a conviction in this case. This is an obvious example of the inadequacy of the old Criminal Code. The problem of course is not confined to teachers, and Parliament has to look to the wider societal problem of child abuse in passing its legislation.

The problem then for teachers is obvious. Any touching of children can be called into question by the mere allegation of one child that he or she has been touched improperly. With the recent energy devoted by schools and social agencies to educate children to come forward when they have been improperly touched, the dangers are increased. This danger is predominantly, if not exclusively, a problem for male teachers in both elementary and secondary situations. One of the popular myths among many teachers is that male teachers only need to be careful in how they handle female students. We have often had teachers describe the extreme care taken whenever they have a female student in a classroom by themselves. However, many of the cases that involve children under 13 concern male teachers touching male students. Teachers must, therefore, be conscious of how they deal with both male and female students.

Innocent touching can potentially lead to a traumatic court experience. In *R. v. C.B.*,[45] a teacher was charged with sexual assault where it was alleged he had touched a female student's left shoulder then moved his hand to her left breast. The judge observed that it would not be unusual for this teacher to put his hand on the student's chair or shoulder when offering assistance in class. He held that the act of touching a student's shoulder was not prudent in today's school setting. He did find that the touching of the student's breast would be inappropriate and subject to a criminal charge. In this case, the teacher was acquitted primarily because the trial judge preferred the teacher's evidence when he denied ever touching the student's breast. The credibility of the witness and the accused is at the heart of these cases.

In another case, *R. v. P.L.S.*,[46] the teacher in question testified that he encouraged children in his class by roughing their hair, patting them on the neck, or back, and placing his hand on their shoulders while complimenting them on their work. He would also squeeze the knees of boys by way of encouragement but he testified that he would never touch girls in this manner. He also claimed that he would put his hand on the neck, elbow, or back of students as a reprimand to guide them back to their seats. He might also have tapped them on the thigh as they were standing at his desk while urging them to think more quickly.

In this case, the teacher was convicted at trial of sexual assault. The trial judge accepted the cumulative evidence of the children and parents as establishing a sexual intent. The conviction was over-turned by the Court of Appeal and acquittals entered on all of the counts because the Court of Appeal found the trial judge erred in examining the cumulative effect of the touchings in looking at intent. The court held that the trial judge should have properly examined each incident individually. The court concluded that the contacts were more in the nature of pats or taps and more likely in the realm of accidental or incidental contact than in the realm of sexual touching. There was no evidence of force or threats and most of the incidents were accompanied by reprimands or compliments in respect to their work. A reasonable observer would not view these incidents as a sexual assault according to the Court of Appeal.

The difficulty of predicting what the courts will do in this new area is emphasized by the restoration of the conviction of the teacher in *R. v. P.L.S.*[47] by the Supreme Court of Canada. The Supreme Court felt that the trial judge had indeed been correct in determining "sexual purpose" in the light of the cumulative evidence of touching. The trauma of being convicted at the trial level and then later having to go to the Court of Appeal must certainly leave its mark. To have the conviction restored by the Supreme Court of Canada would be the final blow. No teacher ever wants to be in that position. Any male teacher reading this account must surely see a part of themselves in the conduct described above. It is almost impossible to teach at an elementary school level and have no contact whatsoever with students. That is, however, clearly where the law is heading. The only direction that can be offered is this: be extremely cautious whenever touching children and avoid any unnecessary contact. Teachers must not conduct themselves as would the parent of the child, but must think of themselves as a teacher in a classroom under the microscope of the law. We can only hope that the law will not prevent teachers from hugging their students when such conduct is appropriate and non-sexual. The educational value may justify the risk in some cases.

In the secondary school setting, the dangers are perhaps a little more obvious. Generally, there is not the same need for touching of students and, therefore, educational problems in restricting touching are minimal. One of the more prevalent problems apparent from the recent case law is that of consensual sexual relations between adolescent girls and male teachers in high schools. Although most teachers agree that this is certainly inappropriate conduct, and teachers' associations and school boards claim it is grounds for discipline and possibly removal of a teacher's licence, it is clear that there are teachers who choose to engage in this activity. In *R. v. Palmer*,[48] a high school teacher was involved in two incidents with female students. The teacher was popular in the school for offering special assistance to vulnerable students and students "at risk." He invited one of these 16-year-old students to his house one evening and engaged in intimate sexual activity. He invited her to go to bed with him but she refused and he took her home.

In the second incident, he was approached by a grade 10 female student who actively pursued an intimate relationship with the teacher. The teacher and student agreed that they would have a sexual relationship but would deny this relationship to anyone who asked. Eventually, the student told her friends of the relationship and rumours circulated around the school. The student attended at the principal's office and denied the rumour, saying that it was entirely her fabrication. The teacher was charged under section 153 of the Criminal Code.

Section 153 of the Code is identical to the sections applicable to sexual touching with the exception that it applies to children over the age of 14 and may only be brought against an individual who is in a position of trust or authority with the child. Teachers obviously fall into this category of persons in a position of trust and authority. The teacher in this case was given a 15-month jail term on conviction.[49] The court stated that the teacher's actions were not only illegal, "but they grossly derogated from his responsibility to direct and nurture the growth of the students both in psychological and physical development." The court further stated:

> In his position of trust, a teacher, like a parent or step-parent, is in a position of dominance over a young person. The teacher has natural advantages of age, experience, finances and probably as important as all of these, a psychological cloak or perception that he is a confidant or a helper to the students who, almost by definition, need that help.[50]

In another similar case,[51] a teacher permitted sexual advances by a 15-year-old student that developed into sexual intercourse on at least six occasions. The court found that parents must be able to trust their children in the care of teachers and not worry about any improper sexual conduct. Teachers who are faced with students who have crushes on them must remind themselves that any intimate activities are totally unacceptable and contrary to the law. In this case, the teacher was not put in prison because the court was further convinced that he had not initiated the conduct and he was remorseful and rehabilitated. The court was convinced that a similar event would not occur again and he was sentenced to one year of probation. This teacher was particularly fortunate in having such a sympathetic trial judge. The court did state that incarceration would be the only appropriate sentence to impose if the teacher had been the instigator of the conduct. We prefer the view that the conduct is reprehensible regardless of who is the instigator.

More typical of the serious consequences for engaging in sexual contact with your students is the B.C. case of *Noyes v. Board of School Trustees, Dist. No. 30 (Caribou).*[52] This case involved a teacher who had sexual relations with students in many different schools before he was finally charged. He suffered legal consequences in both the criminal courts and in the form of a dismissal from his job. His efforts to use section 7 guarantees of fundamental justice in the Charter did not assist him because the court held that its protections did not extend to a livelihood interest. Not only are the legal consequences of engaging in sexual contact with students grave, but the psychological damage to students can be devastating. This is clearly a high-risk activity for teachers in both personal and legal terms.

Duty To Prevent Sexual Abuse

A relatively new area of the law has recently emerged that is a combination of both negligence and criminal law. In *Lyth v. Dagg et al.*,[53] a 22-year-old plaintiff brought an action against a teacher with whom he had been sexually involved when he was 16 years old. The teacher was charged and criminally convicted; as well, a civil court awarded tort damages to the plaintiff for emotional trauma. This case is unique because the student also sued the school board for failing to meet its duty of care. The trial judge summarized the allegation this way:

> The allegation is that the School District knew or ought to have known that Dagg had a propensity to engage in sexual activity with male students and therefore it failed to discharge its duty of care to stu-

dents enrolled in the school when it permitted exposure of adolescent
male students to a teacher with that propensity.

The court heard evidence that three years prior to the initial assault
on the plaintiff, two students had approached the vice-principal of
the school and warned that Dagg was potentially dangerous to male
students. They alleged that they had been to his cabin in Washington
for the weekend and that sexual advances had been made by Dagg.
The vice-principal confronted Dagg with the allegations. He denied
them outright and warned that his solicitors would handle it if the
allegations went any further.

The court found that there was a duty of care on the vice-principal
and school district to protect students from this type of abuse —
particularly when there is some advance warning. In the circumstances, however, the judge was satisfied that the vice-principal had
made the appropriate inquiries and taken reasonable steps to
ascertain whether any real danger existed. In other words, the court
found that the school district had met the appropriate standard of
care. As a legal precedent, this case provides a startling revelation of
the dynamic changes that can occur in the legal process and how the
school environment can be affected by them.[54]

Summary

This chapter has outlined the aspects of a teacher's role that identify
teachers with parents. It is clear from the discussion of the Criminal
Code offences that it is dangerous for teachers to see themselves as
acting in a parental role. At the same time, the common law of
negligence continues to impose the standard of the careful and
prudent parent of which all teachers must be aware; however, that
does not mean that teachers should equate themselves with parents
in the school setting. The reality is that teachers are now viewed as
agents of the state for delivering a service to children and they must
consider themselves as such. Teachers have a range of legal and
professional responsibilities that distinguish them from the parents
of children. We will now move to an examination of that main teacher
role as educational state agent.

ENDNOTES

1. *Jordon House Limited v. Menow and Honsberger* (1973), 38
D.L.R. (3d) 105 (S.C.C.).

2. The "careful parent" rule was first set out in *Williams v. Eady* (1894), 10 T.L.R. 41 (C.A.).

3. Contributory Negligence Act, R.S.N.S. 1989, c. 95; Contributory Negligence Act, R.S.N. 1970, c. 61; Contributory Negligence Act, R.S.P.E.I. 1988, c. C-21; Contributory Negligence Act, R.S.N.B. 1973, c. C-19 (as amended); Negligence Act, R.S.O. 1990, c. N.1; Tortfeasors and Contributory Negligence Act, R.S.M. 1987, c. T-90; Contributory Negligence Act, R.S.S. 1978, c. C-32 (as amended); Contributory Negligence Act, R.S.A. 1980, c. C-23 (as amended); Negligence Act, R.S.B.C. 1979, c. 298 (as amended)

4. *The Times* (London), January 27, 1955; reproduced in G.R. Barrell, *Legal Cases for Teachers* (London: Methuen, 1970), at 245.

5. *Robichaud et al. v. The Queen* (1987), 40 D.L.R. (4th) 577 (S.C.C.)

6. H.C. Cosgrove, "The Teacher and the Common Law," in A. Knott, K. Tronc, and J. Middleton, eds., *Australian Schools and the Law*, 2d ed. (St. Lucia: University of Queensland Press, 1980), at 71.

7. *Beauparlent v. Board of Trustees of Separate School Section No. 1 of Appleby*,[1955] 4 D.L.R. 558 (Ont. H.C.).

8. *Smith v. Martin and the Corporation of Kingston*, [1911] 2 K.B. 775 (C.A.).

9. An example of how far the courts are willing to stretch the scope of vicarious liability may be found in *Moddejonge v. Huron County Bd. of Education* (1972), 25 D.L.R. (3d) 661 (Ont. H.C.).

10. *MacDonald v. Tenbonne Parish School Board*, 253 So. 2d 558 (La. C.A. 1971).

11. *Segerman v. Jones*, 259 A.2d 794 (Md. C.A. 1969).

12. *Snowlake Local Association No. 45-4 of the Manitoba Teachers Society v. School District of Snowlake No. 2309*, [1987] 2 W.W.R. 348 (Man. Q.B.); [1987] 4 W.W.R. 763 (Man. C.A.); leave to appeal to S.C.C. refused, 86 N.R. 400.

13. *Mainville v. Ottawa Board of Education and MacLean* (1990), 75 O.R. (2d) 315 (Sm. Cl. Ct.).

14. *Tommy George v. Board of School Trustees, School District 70 (Port Alberni)* (1986), *School Law Commentary*, Case File No. 2-4-6 (B.C.S.C.).

15. *Board of Education for the City of Toronto v. Higgs* (1959), 22 D.L.R. (2d) 49 (S.C.C.).

16. *Dyer v. Board of School Commissioners of Halifax* (1956), 2 D.L.R. (2d) 394 (N.S.S.C.).

17. *Titus v. Lindberg*, 38 A.L.R. (3d) 818 (N.J.S.C. 1967).

18. See G.R. Barrell, *Teachers and the Law* (London: Methuen, 1978); for case authority see *Mays v. Essex County Council*, cited in Barrell, at 303-6.

19. *Geyer v. Downs* (1977), 17 A.L.R. 408 (Aust. C.A.)

20. *Barnes v. Hampshire County Council*, [1969] 3 L.E.R. 746 (H.L.).

21. *Ramsden v. Hamilton Board of Education* (1942), 1 D.L.R. 70 (Ont. S.C.).

22. *Peter Kelamis v. Board of School Trustees of School District No. 39 (Vancouver)* (1987), *School Law Commentary*, Case File No. 2-5-7 (B.C.S.C.)

23. *Dziwenka v. The Queen*, [1972] S.C.R. 419.

24. *James v. River East School Division No. 9*, [1976] 2 W.W.R. 577 (Man. C.A.)

25. *Donald Brown v. Essex County Roman Catholic School Board, Joseph Carty and Mary Scipione* (1990), *School Law Commentary*, Case File No. 5-5-7 (Ont. S.C.).

26. H. Appenzeller, *Physical Education and the Law* (Charlottesville: Michie Co., 1978), provides a good summary of the basic principles relevant to negligence and physical education as well as examples of the outlandish cases for which the United States is known. J. Barnes, *Sports and the Law in Canada* (Toronto: Butterworths, 1983) is the first comprehensive Canadian book on the topic.

27. There are a number of factors considered; see A.W. MacKay, *Education Law in Canada* (Toronto: Emond Montgomery, 1984), at 124-26.

28. (1968), 64 W.W.R. 301 (S.C.C.).

29. *Myers v. Peel County Board of Education* (1981), 17 C.C.L.T. 269 (S.C.C.).

30. *Thornton v. Board of School Trustees of School District No. 57* (1978), 83 D.L.R. (3d) 480 (S.C.C.).

31. (1975), 57 D.L.R. (3d) 438 (B.C.S.C.).

32. (1976), 73 D.L.R. (3d) 35 (B.C.C.A.).

33. Ibid., at 58.

34. *Myers et al. v. Peel County Board of Education et al.* (1981), 17 C.C.L.T. 269, at 279 (S.C.C.).

35. (1977), 2 C.C.L.T. 269 (Ont. H.C.).

36. (1978), 5 C.C.L.T. 271 (Ont. C.A.).

37. Supra endnote 34.

38. Supra endnote 9.

39. This position is enunciated in *Board of Education for the City of Toronto v. Higgs* (1959), 22 D.L.R. (2d) 49 (S.C.C.), which involved the reaction of a supervising teacher to an accident on an icy playground.

40. *R. v. Dimmel* (1981), 55 C.C.C. (2d) 239 (Ont. Dist. Ct.).

41. *R. v. Bailey* (1986), *School Law Commentary*, Case File No. 1-4-4 (B.C. Prov. Ct.).

42. *R. v. Sweet* (1986), *School Law Commentary*, Case File No. 1-8-1 (Ont. Dist. Ct.).

43. *R. v. Haberstock* (1971, 1 C.C.C. (2d) 433 (Sask. C.A.)

44. *R. v. Cadden* (1989), 48 C.C.C. (3d) 122; 70 C.R. (3d) 340 (B.C.C.A.).

45. (1988), 73 Nfld. & P.E.I.R. 141 (Nfld. Prov. Ct.). It should be noted that this was a charge of sexual assault (s. 271(1)(a)) as opposed to a charge of sexual interference.

46. *R. v. P.L.S.* (1990), 84 Nfld. & P.E.I.R. 181 (Nfld. C.A.). This case also involved a charge of sexual assault (s. 271(1)(a)). The range of sentence for this charge is more serious (life imprisonment) than a charge of sexual interference (maximum of 10 years).

47. As yet unreported at the date of writing.

48. (1990), *School Law Commentary*, Case File No. 5-2-7 (Ont. Dist. Ct.).

49. *Rodney Peter Palmer v. The Queen* (1990), *School Law Commentary*, Case File No. 5-2-7 (Ont. Dist. Ct.).

50. Quoted in *School Law Commentary* Digest, ibid.

51. *R. v. R.B.T.* (1990), *School Law Commentary*, Case File No. 5-9-6 (B.C. Co. Ct.).

52. *Noyes v. Board of School Trustees, Dist. No. 30 (Caribou)* (1985), 65 C.R.D. 400 (10.01).

53. *Lyth v. Dagg et al.* (1988), 46 C.C.L.T. 25 (B.C.S.C.).

54. A similiar case of the "duty to warn" arose outside of the school context in *Doe v. Metropolitan Toronto Police* (1990), 74 O.R. (2d) 225 (Div. Ct.), where the police are being sued by the victim of an assault for not warning of a dangerous sexual offender known to be in the neighbourhood. The case has not yet been decided but the pleadings have been allowed to continue on the basis that they disclose a potential cause of action.

2

Teachers as Educational State Agents

This chapter will review the predominant role of teachers in the schools — that of educational state agents. In the introduction, we reviewed the legal status of teachers and concluded that teachers no longer operate under the *in loco parentis* doctrine but are now more properly considered as agents of the state. This distinction becomes particularly important when reviewing the impact of the Charter of Rights on school teachers. In this chapter, we will discuss the impact of the Charter in some detail, particularly as it relates to making and enforcing school rules. We will also briefly discuss the issue of educational malpractice in Canada.

State Agent — Defined

Most of the education acts across Canada provide some definition of the duties and roles of teachers in the framework of delivering educational services to children. In itself, this is a further indication that the *in loco parentis* doctrine is inoperative. If teachers were truly delegates of the parents, there would be no need for the government to set out a distinct role and duty for teachers because they would simply be required to act as parents. The difficulty with the statutory definitions of teachers' authority is that they are terribly broad, and open-ended. The other major difficulty with these definitions is that in many provinces they have remained largely unchanged over the past 50 years. The provisions in Ontario and Nova Scotia provide good examples of this phenomenon:

The Education Act, R.S.N.S. 1918, c. 9:

s. 93 (1) It shall be the duty of every teacher in the public schools:

(a) to teach diligently and faithfully all the branches required to be taught in the school, and to maintain proper order and discipline therein; ...

(d) to inculcate by precept and example a respect for religion and the principles of Christian morality and for truth, justice, love of country, loyalty, humanity, benevolence, sobriety, industry, frugality, chastity, temperance and all other virtues;

The Education Act, R.S.N.S. 1989, c. 136:

s. 54. It is the duty of a teacher in a public school to:

(a) teach diligently the subjects and courses of study prescribed by or under this Act or the regulations that are assigned to him by the school board;

(b) maintain proper order and discipline in the school or room in his charge ...

(f) encourage in the pupils by precept and example a respect for religion and the principles of Christian morality, for truth, justice, love of country, humanity, industry, temperance and all other virtues;

The Public Schools Act, R.S.O. 1927, c. 323:

s. 100. It shall be the duty of every teacher:

(a) to teach diligently and faithfully the subjects in the public school course of study as prescribed by the regulations, to maintain proper order and discipline in the school; to encourage the pupils in the pursuit of learning; to inculcate by precept and example, respect for religion and the principles of Christian morality and the highest regard for truth, justice, loyalty, love of country, humanity, benevolence, sobriety, industry, frugality, purity, temperance and all other virtues;

The Education Act, R.S.O. 1990, c. E.2:

s. 264. (1) It is the duty of a teacher and a temporary teacher

(a) to teach diligently and faithfully the classes or subjects assigned to the teacher by the principal;

(b) to encourage the pupils in the pursuit of learning;

(c) to inculcate by precept and example respect for religion and the principles of Judaeo-Christian morality and the highest regard for truth, justice, loyalty, love of country, humanity, benevolence, sobriety, industry, frugality, purity, temperance, and all other virtues; ...

(e) to maintain, under the direction of the principal, proper order
and discipline in the teacher's classroom and while on duty in the
school and on the school ground;

Perhaps the most striking feature of these sections is the similarity
between the role defined for teachers in the 1920s and the role as
defined at present. Although teachers in Nova Scotia may take
comfort from the fact that "chastity" and "sobriety" have been
removed in the present Act, the remainder of the definition is
certainly far from comforting. These sections also illustrate that
teachers have good reason to be confused about their role in the
school.

In 1970, Dr. John MacDonald in *The Discernible Teacher*[1] under-
took a study of the teaching profession in Canada at that time. In the
course of this study, he described what he called the "omnicapable
model" of teachers:

The conventional description of the teacher invites teachers to refer
themselves to an omnicapable model, at once intelligent and effectively
warm, knowledgeable and tolerant, articulate and patient, efficient
and gentle, morally committed and sympathetic, scholarly and practical, socially conscious and dedicated to personal development, fearless
and responsible.[2]

Dr. MacDonald's quotation clearly illustrates that the expectations placed on teachers constitute an almost "superhuman" standard. This standard might arguably be the product of the traditional
combination of *in loco parentis* and statutory authority providing an
expanded status for teachers. The two sources of authority combined
provide quite a powerful, almost omnipotent, legal status that may
have spilled over into the definition of a teacher's role. In today's
school setting, this is obviously a dangerous model to follow and at
the very least it is inaccurate and misleading for teachers. It is more
appropriate in today's schools for teachers to think of themselves as
state agents who are small but vital components of a larger educational structure. The statutory definitions of teachers' duties with
their lists of items that are to be "inculcated" or encouraged, by
"precept and example," promote and enhance this omnicapable
myth.

Unfortunately, academic criticism does not change legislative
reality. The reality is that these statutory duties do exist and teachers
should at least be aware of their potential impact. Perhaps a better
definition of the teacher's role and duties may be found in the
professional code of conduct provided by teachers' associations in
each province. These guidelines for conduct provide a more workable

definition upon which teachers may rely in determining their role as state agents. The format of this book does not permit an examination of each of the provincial codes of conduct; however, the reader is encouraged to review his or her code of conduct as a valuable reference. Aside from providing possible role definitions, the teachers' associations in every province have the power and authority to implement disciplinary proceedings in cases where the code of conduct has been breached. It is, therefore, advisable for all teachers to be aware of the provisions of their respective codes of conduct.

Application of the Charter of Rights — Section 32

Having now set the stage for examining teachers in their role as state agents, we can turn our attention to the Charter of Rights and its impact on the school system. The Charter has truly sent a "shockwave" through the education community since its entrenchment in 1982. There are a number of important sections in the Charter that directly affect education as well as how teachers, as state agents, deal with and relate to students. In this section, we will examine the application of the Charter as well as how some of the specific sections of the Charter affect the lives of teachers.

Section 32(1)(b) of the Charter states:

> The Charter applies ... to the legislature and government of each province in respect of all matters within the authority of the legislature of each province.

The Charter can only apply to government action and government actors. It does not regulate the relationship between private individuals. There is no question that the Charter of Rights applies to the education legislation of each province.[3] There may, however, be some question about the scope of the Charter's applications to school boards.[4] There has been some discussion in the case law whether the Charter applies to all school board activity or only to the "government action" type of activity. The Charter, for example, would apply where special education is provided for a particular child; however, it may not apply to a contract for services with a local landscaping company. This has been expressed as delineating between "the nature and quality of the actor" and the "nature and quality of the action or activity."[5] The Supreme Court of Canada has recently reviewed the application of the Charter in the context of education at the university level. In *McKinney v. University of Guelph et al.*,[6] *Harrison v.*

University of British Columbia,[7] *Stoffman v. Vancouver General Hospital,*[8] and *Douglas/Kwantlen Faculty Association v. Douglas College,*[9] the Supreme Court of Canada released concurrently four decisions that relate to mandatory retirement. There were a number of important issues that were canvassed in the 19 separate reasons released by various judges on the four cases; however, one of the important issues for our purposes is the decision that relates to application of the Charter.

The Supreme Court of Canada spent a good deal of time discussing the application of the Charter to university bodies. There were some difficult questions to be addressed given that universities are partially controlled by the government and certainly dependent on government funding; however, they act independently of the government in many respects, including the provision of services to students. The majority of the Supreme Court of Canada consistently found that the Charter did not apply to universities because there was not the requisite quality of governmental control that would justify the application of the Charter. Mr. Justice LaForest qualified this by stating that the court's decision did not preclude the possibility that universities could be found to be part of the government for the purposes of the Charter, but rather that the appellant universities in the present case were not part of the government given the manner in which they were currently organized and governed. The court was also reluctant to apply the Charter in the context of a carefully worked out collective bargaining structure. Both parties had consented to the current employment terms, and the Charter might distort this balance.

There are some important distinctions between universities and school boards that we suggest "tip the scales" in favour of a Charter application to school boards. An education act is specifically aimed at undergraduate education and children are required by compulsory attendance laws to attend school up to the age of 16, in most provinces. Children are not required to attend university. The school board is delivering an educational service that is controlled through provincially developed and approved curriculums. Universities are entitled to set their own curriculums. In many provinces, the school boards are publicly elected similar to municipalities and have taxing powers in some instances. For these reasons, we conclude that although there may be some outstanding questions with regard to a school board's ostensibly non-governmental activity, they will generally be held subject to the Charter. Whenever the educational services to children are affected, the nature and quality of the school board as a government actor and the action it takes will fall under Charter scrutiny.

The more difficult question to answer is whether the Charter of Rights applies to teachers. In *Re Tomen and Federation of Women Teachers Association et al.*,[10] the court held that the Charter did not apply to the collective bargaining arrangements of teachers.[11] Even as public actors, teachers can sometimes be engaged in private matters not covered by the Charter. It is at this point that the *in loco parentis* and statutory powers distinctions become crucial. If teachers were in fact acting *in loco parentis*, they would not be subject to Charter scrutiny because the Charter does not apply to parents. However, given that teachers act as educational state agents pursuant to the statutory authority of the provincial government, there is a convincing argument to be made that teachers are caught in the net of government action for the purposes of Charter application.[12] This does not mean, however, that teachers should expect to be sued personally based on the Charter. The nature of the remedies in the Charter dictate a broader scope of action against school boards or the provincial attorneys general.[13]

The Nature of Charter Rights and Litigation

The Charter of Rights is indeed a unique legal document. It contains a list of rights and freedoms that are to be enjoyed by all Canadians — including children.[14] The Charter is primarily concerned with balancing the rights of individuals against the rights of the collective. In a liberal democratic society where the majority rules, it is a common pitfall that the rights of individuals are often overlooked and overcome by the forces of the state. The Charter is aimed at addressing this potential imbalance. Unlike the Canadian Bill of Rights,[15] the Charter is constitutionally entrenched; this means it is very difficult to amend.[16] It is the entrenchment of the Charter that has led the courts into taking an active role in interpreting the document.

The Charter generally has altered the educational landscape in two significant ways. First, it provides parents with a tool for challenging the substance of school board decisions. Before the Charter, parents were restricted to administrative law remedies that dealt primarily with procedural irregularities.[17] The broad discretion enjoyed by school boards in delivering educational services prior to the Charter is now being eroded.[18] Second, the Charter has national scope. The Charter is the supreme law of Canada and applies to all Canadians. Decisions of the Supreme Court of Canada are binding on all provinces. Therefore, if a Charter issue in education makes its way to the Supreme Court of Canada, the decision of that court will apply to every province whether or not a particular province had any part in the case. Under section 93 of the Constitution Act, 1867, the provinces have always had exclusive jurisdiction in the area of education. The presence of the Charter now makes it necessary for educators to be aware of issues and conflicts in all areas of the country. If, for example, a case involving the religious rights of students arises in Ontario and is decided by the Supreme Court of Canada, it will dictate how students are to be treated across Canada. This is a relatively new phenomenon — one that educators are only beginning to grasp.[19]

Before embarking upon any discussion of the actual content of the rights and freedoms contained in the Charter, it is vital to have an understanding of the actual steps involved in Charter litigation. In many ways, the rights and freedoms are defined by the method and procedures used to enforce these rights. First and foremost, it is important to remember that Charter issues are resolved in the courts following the traditional adversarial approach of courtroom litigation. In other words, it is a lengthy and expensive process.[20]

There are four essential steps to any Charter litigation. First, the court must determine that the Charter, in fact, applies to both plaintiff and defendant in a given case. Second, the plaintiff must make out a *prima facie* (on the face of it) case. Third, the government actor has the opportunity to rely on section 1 of the Charter to limit the rights claimed by the plaintiff. Fourth, the court must determine an appropriate remedy. We will examine each one of these steps.

There are two distinct areas in which the Charter must be held to apply before a case may be heard before the court. First, the defendant must be shown, pursuant to section 32(1)(b) of the Charter, to be a government actor. This was discussed above in the context of education; school boards and teachers will be considered government actors for the purpose of applying the Charter to the educational services provided to children. In relation to other matters, such as collective bargaining, the situation is far less clear.

The second aspect of this first step is that the plaintiff must be claiming a right that is contained in the Charter. The text used in the sections of the Charter is intended to encompass a wide range of rights and freedoms. It is, therefore, not always clear on the face of the section what rights are being protected. There is a strong argument, for example, that section 7 of the Charter, which guarantees to everyone the right not to be deprived of "life, liberty and security of the person" except in accordance with the principles of fundamental justice, creates a constitutional right to an education.[21] Madam Justice Wilson in *R. v. Jones*[22] defined the term "liberty" in the following manner:

> I believe that the framers of the Constitution in guaranteeing "liberty" as a fundamental value in a free and democratic society had in mind the freedom of the individual to develop and realize his potential to the full ...[23]

Clearly, this broad and purposive definition could encompass many aspects of an individual's rights — including the right to an education. We will examine the constitutional right to an education in more detail, later in this chapter.

Once the court is satisfied that the defendant is, in fact, a government actor and the plaintiff is claiming a right that may be included in one or more sections of the Charter, it is then up to the plaintiff to show a "*prima facie* violation" of the rights in issue. There is also the question whether the person claiming the Charter right has legal standing to make the particular claim. If his or her rights have been violated, the court would normally allow the party to have standing. This is a function of the Charter being enforced through the normal course of courtroom litigation. The plaintiff in any civil action has the "burden" to prove its case on a balance of probabilities. In the context of the Charter, the plaintiff is required to show that, "on the face of it" (that is, *prima facie*), his rights under the Charter have been violated. The degree of difficulty in showing this *prima facie* violation will vary depending on the particular facts of the situation and the rights involved.

Some of the sections of the Charter contain "internal limits" that make it more difficult to prove a *prima facie* violation. For example, section 8 of the Charter guarantees that everyone has the right to be secure against "unreasonable" search and seizure. It is not enough simply to show the court that the plaintiff was searched — the search must be shown to be unreasonable before it can satisfy the *prima facie* violation test. Essentially, the plaintiff has the burden, first, to show that his or her fact situation falls within the scope of one of the sections of the Charter and, second, through the introduction of evidence in court, to prove on the balance of probabilities that the rights in question have been violated. The task of gathering, organizing, and leading this evidence in court can be a lengthy and difficult one, thus generating the extensive legal bills mentioned earlier.

Unlike the U.S. Constitution, the Canadian Charter, while protecting individual rights and freedoms, is also an instrument of balance and compromise. This balance and compromise is expressed throughout the Charter; however, it appears most dramatically in section 1:

1. The Canadian Charter of Rights and Freedoms guarantees the rights and freedoms set out in it subject only to such reasonable limits prescribed by law as can be demonstrably justified in a free and democratic society.

This section mandates that all of the rights and freedoms set out in the Charter are subject to "reasonable limits" that are prescribed by the government in an effort to accommodate the interests of all Canadians. In the educational context, it is this section of the Charter that allows school boards to exercise some of the discretion they enjoyed prior to 1982. This section is an expression of common sense for most Canadians, who recognize that for every right there is a corresponding responsibility on some person or agency. Section 1 allows the government to exercise its responsibilities.

The scope of section 1 has been dealt with in detail by Chief Justice Dickson in *R. v. Oakes*.[24] It is unnecessary for present purposes to delve into the elaborate criteria used to test a section 1 limit. Essentially, the court set out three criteria. First, the measures adopted to limit the right must not be arbitrary, unfair, or based on irrational considerations. Second, the means employed should impair as little as possible the right or freedom in question. Third, the effects of these measures must be proportional to the objectives sought in limiting the Charter right or freedom.[25] For school boards, this elaborate section 1 analysis can be avoided by simply asking the questions: "Why do we need this particular rule or policy? What is its effect on the students? Is the rule unfair or arbitrary?" If you are satisfied that a rule or policy is reasonable after asking those questions, you are in a good position to convince a court.

A major stumbling block for school boards is the criterion that, in order to rely on a section 1 limit, it must be "prescribed by law." This does not necessarily require that a limit be set out somewhere in legislation, although this clearly meets the test.[26] In the school context, "prescribed by law" means that school board policies and school rules that limit Charter rights should be in written form and be publicized in some way.[27]

In a Charter courtroom battle where the applicant has proven a *prima facie* violation, the judge will turn to the government actor (that is, the school board) and, before listening to arguments about reasonable limits, ask to see where these limits have been written down. If there are no written limits, the courts are less likely to entertain arguments under section 1. Thus the tendency of many school officials to avoid written rules may have to change. If they do not change, they may be deprived of a section 1 Charter defence.

A further significant feature of section 1 is that it effectively shifts the burden from the plaintiff to the defendant. This can often determine the outcome of a case. The Supreme Court of Canada has established that the burden of showing reasonable limits rests squarely upon those seeking to enforce these limits.[28] In essence, this means that, at the end of the day, if a judge is satisfied that there has been a *prima facie* violation of a Charter right but he or she is uncertain whether or not the government's limits are reasonable, the plaintiff will be successful. More important, even if there is a valid section 1 limit, it may not be recognized by the courts unless it is in some written form.

This requirement represents quite a blow to most school boards and school administrators who often rely on ad hoc policy making. In the areas where Charter violations may arise, proactive decision and policy making will have to replace the previous ad hoc procedures. This should be a prime motivating factor for school boards and school administrators to get together with legal counsel to discuss the policies and practices of the school board and set these out in a clear and accessible written form. Many school boards are already engaged in this process.

Of course, the ultimate goal of any litigation is to obtain an appropriate remedy from the court. In the usual course of litigation this remedy is monetary damages. The Charter has a much broader remedial scope. There are three remedies contained in the Charter. The first is section 24(2), which allows the court to exclude any evidence in a criminal proceeding that has been gathered in a manner that violates the rights in the Charter. For example, a principal who searches a student for narcotics in a manner that violates the Charter may have the evidence found as a result of the search excluded by the courts.[29] We will discuss this issue in more detail in Chapter Three. It is unlikely that section 24(2) could be applied to a disciplinary hearing that concerns students or teachers. There is, however, no binding authority on this point.

The next remedy is found in section 52(1) of the Constitution Act, 1982. This states that the constitution, which includes the Charter, is the supreme law of Canada and any law inconsistent with the provisions of the constitution is, to the extent of the inconsistency, of no force or effect. This section allows individuals the opportunity to have the court strike down a piece of legislation or declare that the legislation is inoperative to the extent that it is inconsistent with a provision in the Charter. This remedy is vital to the integrity of the Charter as a document that sets standards for government action. Again, because the constitution is the "supreme law of Canada," if a section of an education act in one province is struck down by the Supreme Court of Canada, all of the other provinces must take a close look at their own legislation to determine whether or not they have a similar problem.

The final and perhaps most dramatic remedy is contained in section 24(1) of the Charter. This section states:

> Anyone whose rights or freedoms, as guaranteed by this Charter have been infringed or denied may apply to a Court of competent jurisdiction to obtain such remedy as the Court considers appropriate and just in the circumstances.

Because the Charter forces the courts to scrutinize unique and novel situations, the drafters of the constitution realized that they must grant the courts flexible and substantial remedial powers.[30] This is accomplished by section 24(1). In the normal course of litigation, the courts are restricted in their remedies by statutory provisions and principles of common law. These non-Charter remedies may still apply in some circumstances. Section 24(1), however, grants the jurisdiction to the superior courts to step outside the normal restrictions and devise extraordinary remedies.[31]

Plaintiffs are frequently relying on section 24(1) of the Charter in education cases to obtain "interlocutory and interim injunctions." These injunctions are granted before trial to preserve or create a particular status quo for the parties involved. In many jurisdictions, it can take over one year to get to a trial. Some situations demand an immediate remedy. The courts have therefore developed a system whereby they will hear the parties on an interim or interlocutory basis to decide how the situation should be handled until trial. For instance, if a defendant plans to demolish a house and the plaintiff is suing for the ownership of that house, it is vital that the plaintiff obtain an interlocutory injunction to stop the defendant or the trial will be pointless.

Parents are increasingly coming to the courts on an interlocutory basis to have the courts decide Charter issues in education. The test for obtaining an interlocutory injunction is that the plaintiffs must show a "serious issue to be tried"[32] and must show that they will suffer "irreparable harm" if they are not granted the injunction before trial.[33] In many cases an interlocutory injunction will provide a final remedy because, by the time the case reaches trial, the issue has become moot. In *Tuli v. St. Albert Protestant Board of Education*,[34] for example, a grade 12 student was granted an injunction by the Alberta Court of Queen's Bench that allowed him to wear his ceremonial dagger (kirpan) in school. The Human Rights Board of

Inquiry later found that there had been no discrimination but by that time the injunction had lasted long enough for the Sikh student to finish high school.[35]

It is also possible that, where the issue is not moot by the time of trial, the position of the school board has been prejudiced to the extent that there is little likelihood of success. In *Elwood v. Halifax County-Bedford District School Board*,[36] the parents of a 7-year-old mentally disabled child were granted an injunction in October to have their son remain in an integrated setting until trial, which was scheduled to be held in June. The integration of the child over this period of months helped the parents gather evidence on the benefits of integration — evidence that they may not have been able to establish otherwise. The school board decided to settle the case rather than take it to trial.

The threat of an injunction is perhaps one of the most important reasons for school boards to get together with legal counsel to "Charter-proof" their policies and practices. An injunction hearing can be held in most jurisdictions on less than seven days' notice and, as illustrated above, may have the effect of disrupting an entire school year. School boards are particularly at risk if they are taken off-guard and have not turned their minds to the possibility of a Charter challenge. The courts may be sympathetic to the argument advanced by parents that their child will suffer "irreparable harm" if his or her education is affected in some way. The battle will centre around whether or not there is a serious issue to be tried. If school boards address Charter issues and take a proactive stance in clearly setting out their policies and practices, they will stand a much better chance of defending against injunctions. This is particularly so because injunctions are extraordinary remedies and not easy to obtain.

It is perhaps obvious from the above discussion that Charter issues are largely institutional ones and will affect school board policy making and government regulation more than the individual habits of teachers. However, as in all aspects of education, the frontline decisions regarding students are often made by the teacher. Furthermore, teachers are in the best position to bring particular situations in their school to the attention of the superintendents and school board officials. Because teachers ultimately must implement the policies set out by school boards on many of these issues, it is wise for teachers to become more involved as a collective force in structuring some of these policies and procedures. Consequently, it is a good idea for teachers to familiarize themselves with the principles set out in the Charter.

Student Rights under the Charter

One of the thorny problems of applying the Charter to schools is determining who is entitled to exercise these rights — that is, is it the student who claims the rights or the parents on behalf of the student? There are obvious restrictions on the student exercise of rights; however, there are many rights that may be exercised independently. For example, the Young Offenders Act (Y.O.A.) (section 3(e)) provides that children enjoy the independent exercise of all rights under the Charter for the purposes of proceedings under the Y.O.A. This legislation applies to children 12 to 18 years of age. It would be difficult to argue that children are entitled to exercise Charter rights independently for the purposes of the Y.O.A. proceedings but cannot exercise any other rights independently.

The obvious restriction on the independent student exercise of rights is that pursuing any legal redress for a violation requires significant financial resources. Parents normally must support the child if there is to be any means to pursue a legal remedy. However, there are situations — for example, freedom of religion — where the parents' interest and the student's interest may diverge. Throughout this section, we will attempt to identify some of the areas where a divergence between the views of parents and students on the exercise of a particular right may arise. This poses a difficult problem for teachers who may be forced to balance these competing interests.

As we examine some of the various Charter rights that apply to education, it is important to know at the outset that we will not be dealing with two of the larger Charter issues in education given the restrictions of this book. Minority language educational rights, protected by section 23 of the Charter, are an elaborate set of guarantees for protecting linguistic minorities in Canada. This section has been extensively litigated through the courts in the past number of years. However, this is an institutional issue and of minor consequence to individual teachers. In essence, it is up to the provincial governments to determine how they are going to provide minority language education to qualifying parents.

The second issue that we will omit concerns denominational schools in Canada, as protected by section 93 of the Constitution Act, 1867 and section 29 of the Charter. Again, this is a large institutional issue that is primarily of concern to provincial legislators. An examination of these two important Charter issues is beyond the scope of this book because these issues do not significantly affect the various roles of the teacher. The implications of denominational schools for the human and employee rights of teachers will be discussed in due course. These schools also involve the religious rights of students.

Fundamental Freedoms — Section 2

2. Everyone has the following fundamental freedoms:
   (a) freedom of conscience and religion;
   (b) freedom of thought, belief, opinion and expression, including freedom of the press and other media of communication;
   (c) freedom of peaceful assembly;
   (d) freedom of association.

Freedom of Religion

Freedom of religion in the school system has been one of the more widely litigated Charter issues to date. Of course, the freedom of religion for students in a denominational school system, such as that in Newfoundland, is far more circumscribed than in the secular school system. One of the first issues to come to the court based on section 2(a) of the Charter was whether schools could conduct religious exercises in the morning. In *Zylberberg v. Sudbury Board of Education*,[37] a number of parents of non-Christian students challenged a school board policy that required a morning reading of the Lord's Prayer in a grade 2 classroom. The school policy was that any parents who did not wish their child to take part in the exercise could have their child excluded from the class during exercises. The parents challenged this policy on the basis that it was unfair and harmful to their children to force them to be excluded during morning exercises. The parents claimed that the practice should be declared unconstitutional.

At the trial-court level, the court held that although the reading of the Lord's Prayer was a *prima facie* violation of section 2 of the Charter, it was justified as a reasonable limit given the Christian basis of the school system and the fact that students could be excluded at the request of their parents. The Ontario Court of Appeal disagreed with this reasoning and overturned the trial-court's decision. The Court of Appeal determined that the practice was "coercive" and that children at a grade 2 level could not appreciate the "voluntariness" of the practice of allowing them to be excluded from the classroom. The children would only feel singled out and different. The board accepted the ruling and decided not to appeal the case to the Supreme Court of Canada. Consequently, there is not yet a national standard, but the reasoning of the Ontario Court of Appeal is persuasive.

A second issue that was also determined by the Ontario Court of Appeal was that of religious instruction in schools. In *Canadian Civil Liberties Association et al. v. The Minister of Education and the Elgin County Board of Education*,[38] a declaration was sought by the Civil Liberties Association, representing a group of parents in the Elgin County area, that the religious instruction provided by the school board was unconstitutional. There was lengthy evidence presented to the court to explain the religious instruction and its various aspects, which included discussion of religions other than Christianity. The court concluded, however, that the primary purpose of this religious instruction was indoctrination of Christian faith. Part of the evidence was a fill-in-the-blank question on one of the tests in the school that stated: "Jesus Christ is the _____ way to God." The word to be inserted was "only." The Court of Appeal determined that this program was coercive and, therefore, violated section 2(a) of the Charter. The court felt that compelling religious observance through the indoctrination of children cannot be protected by section 1 of the Charter, as a reasonable limit.

In the light of these two decisions, teachers who are providing religious instruction or observing any religious exercises in their classrooms should undertake a careful review of these practices. The clear signal being sent by the Ontario Court of Appeal is that any religious instruction that leans toward indoctrination is coercive and violates the Charter. In many metropolitan school boards, the schools have opted to have religious exercises in the morning that involve readings from various religious faiths. The emphasis is on history and the development of religion as opposed to indoctrination. This may be the wisest course for the future in both legal and educational terms.

Another popular religious issue that has come to the courts in at least two provinces is that of Sikh students' wearing ceremonial daggers (kirpans). Whereas the ideas of religious instruction and exercises involve the school's promoting religion, the issue of the ceremonial dagger involves an individual's claim to exercise their personal religion. In the *Tuli* case,[39] a Sikh student insisted on wearing his ceremonial kirpan on school grounds. The St. Albert school board in Alberta passed a resolution outlawing this practice. This decision was ultimately upheld by the Alberta Human Rights Board of Inquiry, which found that there was no discrimination. In this case, the student argued the relevant provisions of the Alberta human rights legislation rather than the Charter; however, the reasoning would arguably have been similar in either case.

The same issue arose in Ontario in *Pandori et al. v. The Peel Board of Education*,[40] where a Sikh student sought to wear his kirpan at school. A number of compromises were sought between the school and the parents including at one point private instruction for the student in the principal's office, where he could continue to wear the kirpan. Eventually, the student found the situation intolerable and the matter came to a head. A human rights board of inquiry defined the case as a "clash of two rights: the religious freedom of Khalsa Sikhs and the right of the Peel Board to establish disciplinary boundaries and to maximize safety in its realm." The board of inquiry held that the student had the right to wear the kirpan provided that it was of reasonable size, was not worn visibly, and was sufficiently secured so that removal was difficult. The ruling of the board of inquiry was later upheld on appeal by the Ontario Divisional Court.[41] The board of inquiry in Alberta and the courts in Ontario differ on the kirpan issue.

Another interesting example of freedom of religion exercised by students in a school was raised in *Kingston v. Board of Trustees Central Okanagan*.[42] This case involved the indefinite suspension of students who refused on religious grounds to attend coeducational gym classes. In a successful interim-injunction application to return their children to school, the parents established that compulsory participation in coeducational gym classes might be in violation of their rights to religious freedom under section 2 of the Charter. This point was not finally determined because the case did not proceed any further.

This case does raise an interesting potential for student-parent conflict. It is easy to imagine a situation in which the parents, on the basis of their religious beliefs, prohibit their children from participating in coeducational gym classes. The children might not agree. It is conceivable that where the parents have made an arrangement with the school to have their children excluded, a rational 17-year-old student could approach a gym teacher and ask that he or she be allowed to attend the gym class in spite of his or her parents' request. The teacher is then faced with a direct conflict between the student's exercise of his or her independent religious rights and the parents' claim over the religious beliefs of their children. This is a difficult issue to resolve and would have to be settled at a meeting of school administrators, the parents, and the student. It could ultimately be resolved in a court.

Freedom of Expression

There has been no case law to date in Canada directed at the issue of freedom of expression for students in Canada. The leading American case on expression in the schools is *Tinker v. DesMoines*

Independent Community School District,[43] which involved a group of high school students who were suspended for wearing black arm-bands in protest of the Viet Nam war. The U.S. Supreme Court found these suspensions to violate the free speech provisions of the First Amendment and asserted that students do not "shed their constitutional rights to freedom of speech at the schoolhouse gate." There is no reasonable limits clause in the U.S. Constitution; however, the Supreme Court did discuss the limits on students' freedom of speech. The issue was whether the actions of the students created a "material and substantial disruption." The compelling logic of this type of test makes it likely that a similar test may be adopted by Canadian courts.

One of the more prevalent issues that could give rise to a claim to an exercise of freedom of expression is the issue of dress codes in schools. From the questions that we have received at seminars across the country, it appears that many schools have problems with students over the use of profane language on T-shirts, short shorts, halter tops, and wearing hats in school. The only court case on this issue arose with regard to a separate school board in Ontario that implemented a student attire policy that required the wearing of a student uniform. The parents of a number of children brought an application to court to have the policy declared invalid on the basis that it violated the protections of freedom of expression pursuant to the Charter. The Ontario court held that there was no Charter infringement in requiring a student uniform policy. The judge stated that to hold otherwise would trivialize the rights in the Charter.[44]

Generally speaking, schools and teachers will have a wide range of discretion to restrict student expression in the school setting, particularly in cases that relate to dress. A more difficult problem arises in circumstances where a student chooses to have a particular hairstyle — for example, a spiked, red mohawk haircut. While it is possible to change your clothes after school and wear whatever clothing you wish, you cannot necessarily change your hairstyle. A school board may have a difficult time suspending a child for an extravagant hairstyle. Similarly, where students want to run a student newspaper in a high school and the school is reviewing the material with an eye toward censorship, the school personnel should tread carefully but should act appropriately keeping in mind the "material and substantial" disruption test. There is a recent U.S. Supreme Court decision that allows school authorities considerable scope in their censoring of student newspapers. In the pre-Charter case *R. v. Burko*,[45] the Petty Trespass Act prevailed over the rights of former students to distribute literature in the school hallways. It remains to be seen whether a different balance would be struck under section 2(b) of the Charter.

Freedom of Association

This aspect of section 2(d) of the Charter has received a good deal of attention in the field of labour law, but it has had little impact on the field of education. That is not to say that it does not hold the potential for controversy. In fact, one of the early cases on freedom of association was a sit-in by students at the University of Moncton in New Brunswick.[46]

The court held that the group of students who took over the administration building to protest increased tuition fees could not rely on freedom of association because their rights had to be balanced with the rights of others to have unimpeded access to the university. It does not take much imagination to foresee the problems that could arise in the public school context where, for example, high school students wish to form a gay rights club or other sensitive organization. Again, teachers should simply be aware of the reasonable limits section of the Charter and whether they can justify the denial of any such association. There is also the question to what extent schools should lead rather than follow public opinion on matters such as the rights of gays and lesbians. It may also be that the courts would rely on the *Tinker* material and substantial disruption test to apply to the freedom of association issue by analogy.

Special Education

One of the most significant effects of the Charter on education has been in the field of special education. The provisions of the Charter have been seen by parents of disabled children as the means to effecting suitable educational placements and programming for their children. This has been particularly true of the movement toward integrating specially challenged children. The Charter contains two provisions that have an impact on special education:

Section 7:

Everyone has the right to life, liberty and security of the person and the right not to be deprived thereof except in accordance with the principles of fundamental justice.

Section 15(1):

Every individual is equal before and under the law and has the right to the equal protection and equal benefit of the law without discrimination and, in particular, without discrimination based on race, national or ethnic origin, colour, religion, sex, age or mental or physical disability.

Section 15(2):

Subsection (1) does not preclude any law, program or activity that has as its object the amelioration of conditions of disadvantaged individuals or groups including those that are disadvantaged because of race, national or ethnic origin, colour, religion, sex, age or mental or physical disability.

Section 7 of the Charter has been designated as the heart of a constitutional guarantee to education in Canada. Certainly, one can make a strong argument that, in Canadian society today, there is no quality of life, liberty, or security of the person unless a person has a basic education. These arguments are more compelling in the context of the Charter because it expressly guarantees the collective right to education in the context of denominational schools and minority language education in other parts of the Charter. It seems inconsistent to protect specific types of education constitutionally without containing a right to an education itself somewhere in the Charter. It is our view that section 7 does contain a constitutional right to an education but the issue has not yet been decided by the courts. A Newfoundland district court found a right to education in section 7 of the Charter,[47] but it is the only decision of record to date.

The latter part of section 7 focuses on procedural protections and ensures that decisions will be made in accordance with fundamental justice. This has been held to have both a procedural and substantive component but, for now, we will focus on the procedural aspect of this right. In essence, the guarantee is that people should be given a fair hearing by an unbiased decision maker when there are decisions that affect their life, liberty, or security. This emphasis on fair play is particularly important when the classification and placement of a child could have a drastic impact on the rest of his or her life.

In Ontario, there are detailed procedural provisions dealing with both the classification and placement of children with special needs (under Bill 82), and the courts have been reluctant to delve into the merits of a decision or add much to the procedural structure provided by statute.[48] In one early integration case outside of Ontario, *Bales v. Board of School Trustees (Okanagan)*,[49] the judge emphasized that fair procedure in an education context need not be a full-blown court process. This case involved a dispute between school authorities who wanted a mentally disabled child placed in a separate school and the parents who wanted their child in the special education class offered by the regular school. The parents were unsuccessful because they failed to demonstrate that the school's placement was unreasonable.

In *Yarmaloy v. Banff School District No. 102*,[50] the court was more receptive to the parents' arguments about the lack of fair procedure. Although the judge did not reverse the school's segregated placement of the child, he did order that the school authorities conduct a hearing that allows for proper parental input before deciding the issue of the disabled child's placement. In the leading integration case of *Elwood v. Halifax County Bedford District School Board*,[51] procedural irregularities and lack of meaningful parental involvement in the classification and placement of Luke Elwood were essential to the case, which was settled out of court.

For teachers, the significant aspect of the procedural guarantees with regard to special education is that parents should be provided with the appropriate information and notice of the type of classroom setting that can be expected, either in an integrated or special education class. Often the primary responsibility rests with the classroom teacher in an integrated setting to determine whether the child can receive a suitable educational program in a regular classroom. Many teachers voice the concern that the ordinary stresses in a classroom of 25 to 30 children simply do not allow effective teaching of children with special needs. It will be up to teachers to document properly the progress of special-needs children in their classroom so that the parents and the school board have adequate information about the child's program and performance. If the matter were to come before the courts, a judge would be very interested in the classroom teacher's view of the child's abilities and needs.

The equality rights embodied in section 15 of the Charter provide the most substantive weapon for parents in challenging school board authority in the area of special education. There are not many reported cases dealing with section 15 in the context of education as yet because this section of the Charter only came into effect in 1985. Parliament had delayed the enactment of this section for three years to allow provincial governments time to put their legislative houses in order. The Supreme Court of Canada has had the opportunity to review this section (outside the context of education)[52] and has provided some guidance on its interpretation. In essence, the court has determined that not all forms of discrimination will violate section 15. Only discrimination that has an adverse impact on the individual will be subject to Charter scrutiny. Therefore, in the context of special education, the matter becomes a "battle of the experts" to determine whether a mainstream setting or a segregated classroom will have the most beneficial effect on the student. Obviously, the classroom teachers — particularly, special education and resource teachers — will have an important role to play in providing evidence of a child's abilities and suitable programming.

It is important to remember that in any given case, these issues may ultimately be determined in an adversarial litigation process. Referring to our earlier discussion of the steps of Charter litigation, a parent whose child has been segregated into a special education class but who desires a mainstream setting will be required to come to court and show a *prima facie* case of discrimination — including some evidence of adverse impact. Provided that they can show this *prima facie* adverse impact, it will be up to the school board to show the reasonable limits. To do that, the board is well advised to have written policies and procedures for dealing with special-needs children. Teachers can play a vital role in helping to develop these policies and procedures. Many schools and school boards already have these kinds of procedures in place; however, it is important that they now be drafted for scrutiny not only by the parents but by the courts as well.

In the attempt to translate this mass of legal doctrine to the practice of educating disabled children in the schools, three important questions emerge:

(1) Do all disabled children have access to Canadian schools?
(2) What education is appropriate for the disabled child and who should decide this question?
(3) What related services are needed to make access for the disabled meaningful?

Access to the Schools

Except in the cases of severely disabled children, most children now have access to the schools. The general right of access was asserted even before the enactment of the Charter in *Carriere v. Lamont Co. School Bd.*[53] The earlier position was that disabled children were excluded from school because they were a disruptive influence in the class. Even after the enactment of the Charter, the courts have upheld the exclusion of an autistic child from class because the child's behaviour was too bizarre.[54]

Some provinces, such as Nova Scotia, build the potential for exclusion into their statutory framework. Regulation 6(e) under the Nova Scotia statute reads as follows:

> s. 6 Each school board shall provide for all students resident in the area under the jurisdiction of the school board who are entitled to

attend school and who are qualified to pursue the studies in the
grades or courses for which they are enrolled: ...

> (e) special education programs and services to be prescribed by
> the Minister for physically and mentally handicapped students
> between the ages of five and twenty-one who are capable of
> benefitting from such programs and services.

This provision has been criticized as excluding disabled children
without properly establishing what "education" means.[55] It also
seems perverse to exclude a child because the program does not fit.
It appears to us more logical in law and in education to design the
program to fit the child rather than the reverse. There are still
barriers to the physically disabled child because of the costs of
making old school buildings accessible, but progress is being made
slowly. In practical terms, most disabled children do have access
either to schools or to some other appropriate state institution.

Appropriate Education

Establishing the appropriate education for the disabled child leads
directly into the controversy about mainstreaming and integration.
One of the earliest cases on this was *Bales* in British Columbia,[56]
where the segregated placement of the child was upheld. This case
was decided before section 15 of the Charter came into force. In
Hickling v. Lanark-Leeds Roman Catholic School Bd.,[57] the rights of
the parents to have their child integrated into the Catholic school
rather than sent to the special class in the Protestant school was
upheld by an Ontario Board of Inquiry under the Human Rights
Code. This ruling was overturned in the courts at both the trial and
appeal levels because the judges once again deferred to the expertise
of the educators.[58]

The Rowetts, in *Rowett v. The Bd. of Education for York*,[59] took
their fight for the integration of their child to the Special Education
Tribunal in Ontario, but their claim was rejected. The tribunal
refused to consider the arguments based on the Charter, so the
Rowetts went to the courts in an attempt to have their arguments
heard. At the trial level, their case was dismissed on a procedural
point but that ruling has been recently reversed on appeal.[60] The
Rowett case should be heard on its merits sometime within the
coming year. This may be the first direct court ruling on the Charter.

The only case to date in which a child has been integrated as a
result of the Charter is *Elwood v. Halifax County — Bedford Dist.
School Bd.*[61] This is a Nova Scotia case in which Luke Elwood was
integrated for one year by court injunction until the case could be

heard on its merits.[62] Before the case could go to trial on its merits, the parties worked out a detailed agreement that integrated Luke for at least seven years and gave the parents a significant role in his program of studies. It also set up an arbitration structure to deal with disputes and, although not a precedent in the legal sense, it has been widely followed as a matter of practice.[63]

In New Brunswick, there was a successful injunction application at the trial level, under the provincial education statute, to integrate a mentally disabled child. This decision in *Le Conseil Scholaire No. 39 v. Robichaud* was overturned on appeal and the injunction was set aside.[64] With the exception of *Elwood*, the cases to date have not mandated integration of the disabled into the regular classroom. Although the Charter issue has not been squarely addressed in court, judges have shown an inclination to leave the definition of an appropriate education for the disabled in the hands of the educators.

Related Services

In order for the disabled child to benefit from the education provided, there must be related services that allow them to overcome their disability.[65] In respect to the physically disabled, it is essential that transportation and facilities be physically accessible. Accessibility standards are imposed by human rights codes in most of the provinces and the only real resistance to such measures is on the basis of cost.

One of the major areas of concern in integrating the mentally disabled or providing education in a special class is the administration of drugs and medication. Most teachers are not qualified to administer medication or perform medical procedures and by doing this they expose themselves to considerable legal risk.[66] However, if no qualified staff are hired to address the medical needs of these students, they may be effectively excluded from school because of their disability.[67] There are no Canadian cases in which this dilemma has been confronted but it is likely to arise in the near future.[68]

Special education, like minority language education and denominational school rights, is perhaps more of an institutional problem than one directly involving teachers. We have chosen to explain the process carefully here because it has proven itself to be a major concern among teachers. It is now not simply an issue for special education and resource teachers but for every classroom teacher that may be faced with a special-needs child who has been mainstreamed into their classroom. Good school board policies on special education will necessarily involve a frank and open discussion with the teachers in the system to determine the appropriate level of service for students in mainstream classrooms. Teachers should be in a position to understand, at least at an elementary level, the issues and problems facing the school board in this difficult task.

Other Equality Issues

Special education focuses on physical or mental disability as the basis for discriminating against young people in the schools. However, there are also other enumerated grounds in section 15 that could give rise to equality challenges. These have been somewhat lost in the shadow of special education. The Supreme Court of Canada has also made it clear that the enumerated grounds in section 15 are not exhaustive but may be expanded to include other analogous categories. Unlisted grounds in section 15 have been devised to protect the interests represented by other discrete and insular minorities.

Gender

This aspect of section 15 opens up the question whether school policies can validly distinguish between male and female students in the school. This would include things like courses offered only for women or sports teams that are delineated by gender. Outside of the school context, the Ontario Court of Appeal has upheld the right of a teenage girl to play hockey on a boys' all-star team based on section 15 of the Charter.[69] It is important to note from this case that the trial judge accepted the discrimination as justified under section 1 because of the benefits of separating girls and boys in athletic activities. The Court of Appeal disagreed with this reasoning, stating that the section of the Human Rights Code (section 19(2)) that allowed this type of discrimination in athletic activities failed to prescribe any limits or guidelines for the distinction. The court held that participation in athletics is important to the development of "health, character and discipline" and, therefore, worthy of protection. By the time this court case was decided, the young girl in question had moved beyond that level of hockey. This case has, however, paved the way for other women who wish to play male-dominated sports. A grade 12 female student in Kentville, Nova Scotia was recently allowed to play for a male high school hockey team by the Nova Scotia School Athletic Federation. The federation allowed her to play because there was no organized female hockey offered by the NSSAF.[70] In the high school setting, teachers may have to pay attention to the bases for distinguishing coeducational and non-coeducational gym classes as well as the restrictions on women playing male-dominated sports.

Age

The primary issue in the field of age discrimination will be whether the age limits for starting and finishing public education are reasonable. For young children, problems are most likely to arise in cases where parents feel that their child is particularly gifted and the "appropriate" education should consequently begin at an early age. In *Winnipeg School Division No. 1 v. McCarthur*,[71] the parents tried to force a school to admit their child who was one month short of the required five years of age at the cut-off date. This case was heard before the Charter's enactment and the parents employed the Human Rights Code of Manitoba. The court held first that the human rights legislation did not apply to schools. More important, however, the court held that the age restrictions in the education act were specific and had been enacted later than the human rights statute; hence, the age limitation prevailed. This illustrates that the courts may rely on the reasonable limits section in the Charter of Rights to limit claims of age discrimination in relation to early school admission.

In one school board in Quebec, administrators ran into a "slippery slope" problem of trying to assess each child individually for the appropriate entry age for primary education. The school board developed a policy in which parents could attend a meeting of a committee set up by the school board to assess a child's abilities and whether it would be appropriate for that child to start school earlier than the prescribed cut-off date. This process involved gathering and bringing evidence before the school board of the child's ability, which was a costly exercise. The board consequently found that it was only parents of higher economic means that were applying. The board was then faced with a difficult universality dilemma; their new program was effectively excluding lower-income children. It may be that schools should not try to enter into this kind of inquiry but should simply rely on the traditional means of setting an arbitrary cut-off date. The courts are likely to defer to a school board's cut-off date provided that the board can show some reasonable basis for limiting the access of young children.

A far more contentious aspect of age discrimination under the Charter is the extension of educational services to adults. Each provincial education act contains various provisions that pertain to the cut-off age for publicly funded education. Many of these statutes also include special provisions for adults in the education system. In British Columbia and in the Northwest Territories, for example, there are different procedures for the suspension and expulsion of students who are over the age of 18. This kind of statutory discrimination is certainly open to challenge. The extension problem is particularly acute in cases where a disabled student needs special education services past the age of 21.

A variation on this theme occurs in the North, where aboriginal people often decide to return to school later in life. Given their differing cultural values, there is a strong argument to be made that the age limitation for aboriginal people should be more flexible. As yet, these cases have not found their way into the courts. The argument on behalf of aboriginal people becomes stronger when coupled with a further argument under section 15 that restricting access to schools is a matter of race discrimination. In fact, age limits are a good example of structural or systemic race discrimination that is not obvious at first glance. Racial discrimination is most often a problem of latent structural inequalities.

Race

The systemic nature of race discrimination makes it difficult to attack on an individual-case basis in the courts. In spite of this, there have been some human rights challenges but in most instances the cases do not even proceed to a board of inquiry let alone the courts. The primary reason for these settlements is the desire on the part of school boards to avoid the negative publicity that accompanies a racial complaint. Although race and ethnic origin are explicitly included in section 15 of the Charter, there have been no cases to date that have proceeded to trial.

Complaints of racism are most likely to be coupled with an argument under section 27 of the Charter, which protects the multicultural heritage of Canadians:

> Section 27. This Charter shall be interpreted in a manner consistent with the preservation and enhancement of the multicultural heritage of Canadians.

It should be noted that this is an interpretive section and does not contain the same substantive force as some of the other provisions of the Charter. Most provinces, however, have multicultural policies with respect to education and this section may be used as a means of strengthening the application of these provisions. Because of the wide scope of these racial issues and the systemic nature of the discrimination, it is perhaps a problem that is beyond the means of any one teacher to correct. It is, however, important for all teachers to be aware, as educational state agents, of potential discrimination in their schools — particularly latent or systemic discrimination. On a very practical level, all teachers in elementary school grades should take a close look at the materials they are teaching in their classrooms for outdated racial references. Teachers should also be sensitive to their own biases.

Enforcing School Rules in the Wake of the Charter

The foregoing discussion focused on potential Charter problems in the delivery of educational services. There are a host of separate Charter issues that primarily involve school discipline and the making and enforcement of school rules. Obviously, all aspects of the school system hierarchy are involved in the discipline process, from provincial department officials through to school board members and administrators down to the classroom teacher. For teachers to understand their role properly, it is important to take a bird's-eye view of the whole rule enforcement process.

The school rule process can be broken into three phases:

(1) making rules;
(2) enforcing rules; and
(3) penalizing for breach of rules.

Given this breakdown, the board can be viewed as a microcosm of the larger political structure:

(1) rule making is a legislative function;
(2) rule enforcing is an administrative function; and
(3) penalizing is a judicial function.

All rungs of the school hierarchy are involved in rule making at different levels. It is education department officials and school board members who spend most of their time formulating policy and drafting rules. School administrators and teachers are the primary rule enforcers and in some respects resemble a school police force. We will deal with the police aspect in the next chapter. Finally, it is school administrators and school board members, as well as committees composed of both, who normally sit in a judicial capacity and determine the penalty for breach of a particular rule. The compartments are far from watertight because teachers and administrators may also get involved in rule formulation or the assessment of penalties. It is important to consider which of the rule-related functions is related to a particular set of facts because there are different Charter considerations for each function.

Rule Making

At the rule-making level, the major Charter concern is with the actual content or substance of the rules. Rules that in substance violate principles contained in the Charter may be subject to challenge. We have already looked at many of the substantive aspects of the Charter that can affect the delivery of education. School rules similarly would be subject to scrutiny if they were restricting, for example, freedom of expression or freedom of speech. One of the examples referred to earlier was school dress codes, which might arguably be seen to violate a student's freedom of expression. School officials should look at the school rules from a "reasonable limits" perspective. Whether or not there are Charter violations, it is a useful exercise for schools to look at all of their rules to see which ones are reasonable.

As mentioned earlier, the burden of showing that a particular rule is a reasonable limit on a Charter right rests clearly with the state agent who made the rule or seeks to apply it. This is done through the operation of section 1 of the Charter. In the school context, this means the school board, school administrator, or teacher must "demonstrably justify" the rule as a reasonable one in a free and democratic society. This, in essence, involves asking the questions: Why do we need this particular rule? What is its effect on the students? Is the rule unfair or arbitrary? In addition to answering these questions, the school officials will have to bring forth some convincing evidence to show why the objective of the rule could not be achieved without violating a Charter right. The Supreme Court of Canada has set a further requirement for section 1 — the means used to sanction a particular behaviour must be reasonable and proportional to the ends sought.[72]

Another limitation on the use of section 1 of the Charter to justify a school rule is that the rule must be "prescribed by law." This means that it must be clear enough to allow students to understand when their conduct would violate the rule. It must be communicated in a clear and accessible form. In practical terms, this means that school board policies and school rules must be in written form and publicized in some way.[73] The safest course is to have the rules codified and distributed to both parents and students at the beginning of the school term. In many cases, a thoughtful review of rules will allow educators to avoid any conflict in the first instance by "cleaning their own house." Being proactive rather than reactive is the key to avoiding Charter challenges.

Teachers have their "finger on the pulse" of students because of their frontline contact. It is vital, therefore, that teachers take an active role in the formulation of school rules. We recommend, that as part of the year-end process in June of each year, the teachers set aside one morning or one afternoon to go through the school rules and determine whether any of them need amending or updating. It may also be a useful exercise to have the student councils or other representative groups of students brought in as part of this process. Certainly, schools should get into the habit of formulating and distributing a school policy handbook to students at the beginning of each year. This will avoid a great deal of conflict with both students and parents and may be seen as a good educational as well as legal practice. Fair process should be taught by example as well as precept.

Enforcing Rules

Although rule making is fairly distinct from the other two categories, the line between administratively enforcing the rule and judicially setting the sanction is much less clear. This is largely because the same people are often involved in enforcing the rule and deliberating on the penalty. In the larger society, there is a clear line between the police who enforce the laws and the judges who handle the sentencing. In the school setting, however, the principal may be the person who makes the rule, enforces it, and penalizes those who break it. Often there is no clear line between each of these different roles.

In the next chapter, we will discuss in detail the teacher's role as "police state agent." In enforcing school rules, often the line between an educational state agent enforcing rules and a police agent enforcing the criminal law becomes blurred. That is primarily because many school problems span both areas. The current trend in schools is to rely more heavily on the criminal law in cases where students have committed a clear breach of the law. In the past, the "paternal" tendencies of educators led them to deal with some of these problems on an in-house basis. This has been replaced by a more standard reliance on criminal procedures in many schools. The Young Offenders Act (Y.O.A.) has also mandated that teachers and administrators clearly delineate between whether they are enforcing a school rule or whether they intend to use the criminal process. The evidentiary restrictions created by the Y.O.A. do not apply to school rules. We will examine these evidentiary restrictions in more detail in the next chapter. For now, we will look at the enforcement of rules through the in-house school process.

It is easy to think of school rules that in their content do not violate the Charter but could be applied in a manner that does violate the Charter. A rule that states that no student or teacher may smoke in class does not discriminate on its face. If the rule is applied only to males or only to students in grade 11, there may be grounds for an equality challenge. This is a problem of application and not content.

A more likely problem is the procedure by which rules are enforced. Although many provinces have adopted a detailed procedural code, other provinces such as Manitoba, Newfoundland, New Brunswick, and Prince Edward Island give students very few procedural rights. Some of these provinces may fall short of the fundamental justice guarantees contained in section 7 of the Charter.

Section 7 has both procedural and substantive content. This means that it may be used to challenge both the content and the procedure of government action. Thus, it could be used as the basis for a challenge to a rule based on "vagueness" where the rule is not sufficiently clear to provide proper notice of its content. It also imposes a constitutional form of Canadian due process.

In applying section 7 to the school context, we are assuming that education is encompassed within the phrases of "liberty and security of the person." There could also be simple cases of detention in the school context that would attract section 7 procedural protections. In essence, schools may not deprive a student of his or her "liberty" (that is, education) without following some form of due process. This due process will be less than full court procedures; however, it necessarily involves giving the student some notice of the rule involved, the opportunity to be heard at some point, and the right to know the case against him or her. Those provinces that have a detailed code of procedures for suspension and expulsion would be likely to meet the section 7 standard, with the possible exception of those that allow only for *post facto* hearings for the student. In some cases, a pre-suspension hearing may be appropriate, even if it is only an informal discussion in the principal's office. Those provinces with no procedural guarantees are unlikely to meet the section 7 standard.

The necessity of due process in the schools is illustrated by a Nova Scotia case, *Re M.B.*,[74] in which a teenage girl was suspended from high school and placed in a private school by the Children's Aid Society, because she was allegedly "unmanageable." Under the existing section 55(1) of the Children's Services Act, the court held that this placement violated section 7 of the Charter because the girl was not provided with the dates, locations, and specific instances of her alleged unmanageability, to allow for a proper defence. It is a commonly held principle of fundamental justice that accused persons have the right to know the case against them.

In a more recent decision, the New Brunswick Court of Appeal upheld the expulsion of a student who had violated the school's no-smoking rule for a third time.[75] On the first infraction, he and his parents had been informed of the rule and, on the second, he had been suspended for three days. The student was expelled by the principal for the third infraction, and this decision was supported by the school board at a meeting attended by neither the parents nor the student. The student obtained an interlocutory injunction to force the school board to reconvene and consider the matter with proper representations.

The board met a second time, examining affidavits from students and teachers and allowing the student, his parents, and his lawyer to make representations; the expulsion was upheld. The student appealed further to the Queen's Bench for reinstatement and damages, but the action was dismissed. This decision was appealed and dismissed by the Court of Appeal, which held that the interlocutory motion should never have been granted because the student did not have a "real prospect of succeeding" at a trial. In spite of this final ruling, which is based primarily on the legal complexities of interlocutory motions, this case underscores the requirement for school boards to act fairly and in accordance with the principles of fundamental justice when they are suspending students. If the school board had initially put procedures in place that accorded with section 7 of the Charter, they might have avoided this time-consuming and costly litigation.

In terms of allowing proper presentation of a case before the school board, it is important as a classroom teacher to be aware of these potential difficulties and to document incidents properly. As was seen in Re M.B., the challenge under section 7 of the Charter was primarily based on improper documentation of the events to the extent that the student did not have proper notice of the case to be met. These documentation issues raise the problem of maintaining proper student records in the schools. All of the provincial education acts require that records be kept that contain all information relevant to the improvement of the instruction of those pupils. A detailed review of student record issues is beyond the scope of this book because this is an institutional issue for administrators and provincial policy makers to determine. However, certainly as a temporary measure, teachers should be encouraged to note student behaviour and perhaps place it in a portion of a student file that can be removed once the discipline issue has been dealt with.

Aside from the Charter, there may be a further statutory requirement to keep proper notation of student behaviour for a potential suspension or expulsion hearing. For example, the Nova Scotia Education Act requires a student to be "persistently disobedient" in order to be expelled. Similarly, in Ontario, the Education Act states that a student's behaviour must be "refractory" (which is defined as "persistently disobedient") for the student to qualify for a suspension. In *Re Peel Board of Education et al.*,[76] the court was faced with an expulsion hearing for a student who had been charged under the Y.O.A. The judge held that the hearing could not go forward for reasons that we will detail in the next chapter. However, important for present purposes were his comments that one incident of misbehaviour probably did not constitute "refractory" behaviour for the purposes of the Education Act. It is necessary under the provisions of the Act to show a history of disobedience for the school board to meet the statutory standards.

Penalizing for Breach of Rules

Although most sanctions can be challenged as infringing a liberty or security interest under section 7 of the Charter, judges will not ban all forms of discipline in the schools. Thus, suspensions, fines, and the recording of negative comments in student records are likely to be acceptable as long as they are enforced fairly. Similarly, detentions are likely to be acceptable if they are not so long in duration as to constitute cruel and unusual treatment under section 12 of the Charter. Some jurisdictions, such as British Columbia, have solved this problem by establishing statutory maximums (for example, 30 minutes) in their regulations on detentions. The trend in many schools across the country now is toward "in-school suspensions." Rather than holding children after school or during lunch hour, schools have opted for in-school suspensions ranging from one to three days as a more effective means of discipline. This type of educational policy will not likely be considered to violate provisions of the Charter.

The critical Charter section with regard to penalizing for breach of rules is section 12:

> Section 12 — Everyone has the right not to be subjected to any cruel and unusual treatment or punishment.

The first question to be considered is whether section 12 of the Charter applies to schools at all. In the United States, the cruel and unusual provision was not applied to schools.[77] The U.S. Supreme Court restricted the provision to criminal matters. One reason for this approach was that the historical context and the old statutes on which the amendment was based indicated to the court that it was intended to protect criminals from abuse. This reasoning is reinforced by the reference to excessive bail and fines as well as to the use of the word "punishment."

It is possible to argue in the Canadian context that section 12 of the Charter is potentially stronger because it does not have the same origins as the U.S. Eighth Amendment and because there is no reference to bail or fines that would limit it to the criminal context. It may also be significant that the word "treatment" as well as "punishment" is used in the Charter. The word "treatment" has a broader meaning than the word "punishment" and has less criminal connotation. On this basis, it is possible that a Canadian court might find that section 12 of the Charter does prevent school officials from subjecting students to cruel and unusual punishment or treatment. The issue is likely to boil down to a section 1 analysis of whether the treatment or punishment used is "reasonable" in the circumstances.

Most penalties could be administered in a way that violates the cruel and unusual provision. However, the concern of this section will be penalties that, by their substantive nature, could violate section 12. The most logical candidate for concern, as mentioned earlier, is corporal punishment. Corporal punishment has largely been taken out of the schools in most jurisdictions in Canada. Where it is used, it is primarily at the discretion of the principal rather than the individual teacher. One significant guideline for section 12 may be found in the Supreme Court of Canada's discussion of section 43 of the Criminal Code.[78] Former Chief Justice Dickson stated that before looking at whether the force was reasonable in the circumstances, it would be necessary to show that the person applying the force intended it for "correction," and that the person being "corrected" was capable of learning from the correction. This case arose in the context of a counsellor using force by way of correction (that is, tapping a spoon on the student's forehead) at an institution for mentally handicapped adults. The court found that the correction in the circumstances would not be defensible under section 43 of the Code because the student was incapable of learning from the correction, since the student had no recollection of the event one or two minutes after it occurred.

Generally speaking, the same analysis may be expanded to cover issues under section 12 of the Charter. Anytime a teacher is imposing a form of treatment or punishment on a student, one consideration should be whether the discipline is appropriate in the circumstances and whether the child can appreciate the nature of the discipline. Obviously, teachers in special education settings will have to pay particular attention to their handling of students because of the potential lack of appreciation by the individual student. Where possible, the discipline procedures of the school should be set out in writing in a school policy handbook so that the defences available under section 1 (reasonable limits) will be readily ascertainable to a court. There has been at least one case to date in which section 12 was used by the courts to invalidate a provincial education statute. In *R. v. B.M.*,[79] section 12 of the Charter was used to strike down the truancy provisions of the Education Act in Nova Scotia. The court found that the procedures followed under the Act did not meet the requirements of "fundamental justice" in section 7 and that the imposed indefinite sentence to a reformatory violated section 12 of the Charter. As a response to this decision, the Nova Scotia government amended the Education Act to take truancy outside the criminal context altogether. It is now a matter for social services, and truancy may be one factor in a child protection proceeding. This process of court challenge followed by legislative reform may become a familiar pattern for changing rules with unfair procedures and excessive punishments.

Educational Malpractice

Given the "rights consciousness" of parents and the general tendency toward increased use of the courts by parents, educational malpractice has become a popular topic of discussion among educators and academics. We have chosen to discuss malpractice in this chapter rather than in the section on negligence because liability for educational malpractice is often the result of an institutional failure rather than the result of one teacher's negligence. Of course, a claim of educational malpractice might arise from the misclassification of a student by one particular teacher. However, it will generally be the institution as a whole that fails to pick up this misclassification as the child moves through the system that would give rise to a claim for educational malpractice.

Although this is a popular discussion, it is our opinion that there is actually little chance of success of any educational malpractice action in Canada. It is simply not a recognizable tort in the Canadian courts. The U.S. courts have displayed an extensive history of avoiding the imposition of a duty on the public education system, which would give rise to damages for educational malpractice. Unlike other forms of professional negligence that will provide an action in tort, the U.S. courts have held that the state is conferring a benefit upon people through education and therefore it is against public policy to hold them liable in negligence.[80] The only exception to this rule has been some extraneous judicial comment that the court might intervene in the most exceptional circumstances involving "gross violations of defined public policy."[81]

There is some trend toward allowing an educational malpractice claim in cases where it can be framed as medical malpractice. In *Snow v. The State of New York*,[82] for example, a deaf plaintiff was improperly diagnosed as retarded and placed in state schools for the mentally handicapped. The court upheld his claim for $1.5 million in damages as "medical malpractice." At the same time, the court rejected the claim of Frank Torres, a ward of the state, who was treated in a similar manner because no one recognized that his poor test results arose from his inability to speak English properly. This provides a good illustration of the U.S. courts' failure to impose a duty on educators in the area of malpractice.

In Canada, perhaps the most notable educational malpractice case to date involved an outright rejection of educational malpractice as a cause of action in Canada. In *Hicks et al. v. The Board of Education for the City of Etobicoke and the Durham Board of Education*,[83] the parents claimed that the school board owed a duty of care to their child, which the board breached by failing to provide proper education and instruction. The parents sought damages for developmental harm and for mental anguish and embarrassment as well as out-of-pocket expenses for private tutoring.

Before the matter could even proceed to any stages of litigation or trial, the school board brought an application to have the statement of claim dismissed as disclosing no reasonable cause of action. The court allowed the application and dismissed the statement of claim. The court stated that there are no authorities in Canada that recognize educational malpractice as a tort. The U.S. authorities, furthermore, have consistently held that a cause of action for damages for negligence in the educational process is precluded by major considerations of public policy.

We think that the more appropriate attack on the issue of educational malpractice from the parental standpoint is a proactive rather than a reactive action. The courts are clearly disinclined to award monetary damages to children after the fact — that is, there will be no cause of action for parents to come to the courts with a 17- or 18-year-old child and say that he or she has been improperly educated and, therefore, they should be given some large sum of money to compensate for the loss.

The courts will be more inclined to entertain an action by parents in the early stages of their child's education to have an appropriate education given to their child pursuant to the Charter and the duties of school boards under the education acts. This can already be seen in some of the Charter challenges to segregated special education classes. Parents who feel that the appropriate education for their child is in a mainstream setting — such as the parents in the *Elwood* case — have a much better chance of success by pursuing the matter when their child is young rather than coming to the courts 10 years later and looking for monetary damages to compensate for what they feel was an inappropriate education.

Teachers should be aware of the spectre of educational malpractice, "à la medical malpractice" as found in the U.S. courts. There is also the potential for legal trouble where a child is inappropriately assessed by such school personnel as school psychologists, who cross the line between education and medicine. It would still be a difficult case for the parents to make out in court; however, under the U.S. authorities, these avenues may still be open. In general, there need be little fear among teachers of facing educational malpractice suits in Canada.

Copyright

The area of copyright law in Canada is a difficult topic even for lawyers. The area has become even more confused and controversial in recent years by the introduction of Bill C-60 in the spring of 1987. This legislative enactment was the first attempt by the government to alter the traditional protection of copyright in Canada.

Given the complex nature of this area of the law, a proper review is beyond the scope of this book. Any discussion on teachers and the law would, however, be incomplete without some mention of the perils of the photocopier and the videotape machine.[84]

Traditionally, Canadians have not truly understood the legal reality of copyright protection. Although many of us would not consider stealing vegetables from our neighbour's garden, we would not hesitate to videotape our favourite television program, tape a CD belonging to a friend, or photocopy an interesting article from a periodical or newspaper. Under the law, these violations are just as illegal as any other kind of stealing.

One of the major problems with the protection of copyright is that legislators are simply unable to keep up with technological advances. The first commercially successful photocopy machine was not available until 1959 and photocopying did not really come into vogue until the 1970s. Similarly, videotape machines and good-quality cassette recorders are a phenomenon of only the last 15 to 20 years.

Section 3(1) of the Copyright Act currently sets out the rights that belong to a creator:

> 3(1) for the purposes of this Act "copyright" means the sole right to produce or reproduce the work or any substantial part thereof in any

material form whatever, to perform, or in the case of a lecture to deliver, the work or any substantial part thereof in public or if the work is unpublished, to publish the work or any substantial part thereof, and includes the sole right

(a) to produce, reproduce, perform or publish any translation of the work,

(b) in the case of a dramatic work to convert it into a novel or other non-dramatic work,

(c) in the case of a novel or other non-dramatic work, or of an artistic work, to convert it into a dramatic work, by way of performance in public or otherwise,

(d) in the case of a literary, dramatic or musical work, to make any record, perforated roll, cinematograph film or other contrivance by means of which the work may be mechanically performed or delivered,

(e) subject to subsection (2), in the case of any literary, dramatic, musical or artistic work, to reproduce, adapt, and publicly present the work by cinematograph, if the author has given the work an original character,

(f) in the case of any literary, dramatic, musical or artistic work, to communicate the work by radio communication,

(g) to present at a public exhibition, for a purpose other than sale or hire, an artistic work created after the coming into force of this paragraph, other than a map, chart or plan or cinematographic production that is protected as a photograph,

and to authorize any such acts.[85]

The defences to copyright infringement are contained in section 27(2) of the Copyright Act, which lists a number of exceptions to the infringement, the most important of which for educators is paragraph (a) that states:

(a) any fair dealing with any work for the purposes of private study, research, criticism, review, or newspaper summary.[86]

This concept of "fair dealing" should not be confused with the American developments with regard to a "fair use" of copyright. These U.S. rules have largely contributed to Canadian teachers' misunderstanding of copyright law. In the United States, the Copyright Act allows teachers the right of "fair use" to make:

(a) for their personal use in teaching of research, single copies of a chapter of a book, an article from a periodical, a short story or poem,

(b) for classroom use by students, multiple copies of the same work, subject to criteria such as brevity, spontaneity, and cumulative effect.

This notion of fair use has been considered and rejected by the federal government in Canada. Therefore, under the Canadian statutory definition of "fair dealing," teachers do not enjoy the same protection as their American counterparts.

Another significant cause of misunderstanding among teachers is the terribly ineffective policing of copyright laws in Canada. Because of the way copyright law is structured, it is up to the individual creator or author of a work to undertake enforcement. The federal government has set up the law but there are very few cost-effective mechanisms for enforcement.[87] Traditionally, it has been very difficult for anyone to take effective action against infringement. In the musical sphere, the Society of Composers, Authors, and Music Publishers of Canada (SOCAN) has served a useful role for songwriters in enforcing copyright infringement and in securing licences from all users of musical works. Unfortunately, this has not been true of authors of literary works.

The Copyright Act is being amended in two phases. Phase one has been completed and the legislation now deals more thoroughly with violations of software "pirating" and skirts some of the difficult issues such as fair dealing and educational and library exemptions. As a result of phase one, the Canadian reprography collective (Cancopy) was incorporated as a non-profit organization in the summer of 1988 to represent the interests of publishers and authors. In March 1989, Cancopy contacted all ministers of education in Canada and asked them to commence negotiations for provincial licences. The thrust of the negotiation was to follow the similar path taken by SOCAN in the musical sphere by licensing schools and school boards to allow for blanket exceptions for copyright. Reproductions are to be monitored and the proceeds from the licences to reproduce distributed to the authors of various works.

This negotiation is very difficult without Parliament's taking any action on phase two of the Copyright Act. The provinces are reluctant to negotiate any licences with Cancopy until they are aware of what exemptions might be available for library and educational institutions. In the spring of 1991 these exemptions were soundly rejected by the creative community and there are currently strong lobbying efforts on both sides being made for the language of these exemptions. There are, as yet, no deadlines for the drafting and implementation of phase two.

At present, therefore, teachers are at risk whenever they use a photocopier or a videotape machine. This is an unfortunate situation given that many of our best creative teachers are the ones who are constantly on the lookout for current topical information to supplement their course materials. However, the policing of copyright infringement remains as ineffective as always and, therefore, the risk of an actual lawsuit is minimal. No school board, however, wants to be caught out and held up as an example by an author in order to get Parliament to move more quickly on their legislative amendments for phase two. For now, we recommend that teachers stay in close contact with their provincial government authorities responsible for negotiating with Cancopy. The situation changes monthly and the extent of photocopy licences could easily vary from province to province.[88]

Summary

As illustrated in this chapter, the teacher's role as an educational state agent is a complex one. As a vital component of the larger institutional structure, teachers are required to be more aware of all of the issues surrounding the delivery of educational programs in Canada. As a frontline contact with students, teachers have a responsibility to make themselves aware of issues, and when they find new issues arising in their day-to-day activities, they should bring these to the attention of administrators so that effective policies can be put in place to deal with these matters. Perhaps the most important thing to remember is that the educational state agent role of teachers should be their primary role. Gone are the days of the parental delegation and it is more important now for teachers to see themselves as one significant component of a larger institutional structure.

ENDNOTES

1. John MacDonald, *The Discernible Teacher* (Ottawa: Canadian Teachers Federation, 1970).

2. Ibid., at 4.

3. See the recent decision of the Supreme Court of Canada in *Mahe et al. v. Alberta* (1990), 105 N.R. 321.

4. See for example *Zylberberg v. Sudbury Board of Education* (1988), 65 O.R. (2d) 641 (C.A.).

5. *Re Ontario English Catholic Teachers' Association et al. v. Essex County Roman Catholic School Board* (1987), 36 D.L.R. (4th) 114 (Ont. H.C.).

6. *McKinney v. University of Guelph et al.* (1990), 118 N.R. 1 (S.C.C.).

7. *Harrison v. University of British Columbia*, [1991] 1 W.W.R. 681 (S.C.C.).

8. *Stoffman v. Vancouver General Hospital*, [1991] 1 W.W.R. 577.

9. *Douglas/Kwantlen Faculty Association v. Douglas College*, [1991] 1 W.W.R. 643.

10. *Re Tomen and Federation of Women Teachers Association et al.* (1987), 61 O.R. (2d) 489 (H.C.J.).

11. Ibid.

12. Justice Grange of the Ontario Court of Appeal in *R. v. J.M.G.* (1986), 56 O.R. (2d) 705, at 708, stated that he was prepared to assume that "the school board directing the affairs of the school and the school itself, including the principal and the other teachers are subject to the Charter in their actions and dealings with the students under their care."

13. Teachers are also protected against personal lawsuits in the school context by the doctrine of vicarious liability: see A.W. MacKay, *Education Law in Canada* (Toronto: Emond Montgomery, 1984), at 133; see also the discussion on remedies, infra.

14. It is not clear at exactly what age children will attain the independent exercise of their Charter rights; however, the Young Offenders Act, R.S.C. 1985, c. Y-1 (section 3(e)), bestows "special guarantees" of Charter rights upon children over the age of 12 and allows for the independent exercise of these rights.

15. Canadian Bill of Rights, R.S.C. 1970, Appendix III.

16. Amendment requires the assent of two-thirds of the provinces with 50 percent of the population and the consent of both federal houses.

17. See *Ward v. Board of Blaine Lake School*, [1971] 4 W.W.R. 161 (Sask. Q.B.).

18. For examples of the courts sustaining this broad discretion, see *Re: Robertson and Niagara South Board of Education* (1973), 41 D.L.R. (3d) 57 (Ont. H.C.); and *Crawford v. Ottawa Board of Education*, [1971] 2 O.R. 179 (C.A.).

19. For a more detailed discussion of this phenomenon, see Terri Sussel and Michael Manley-Casimir, "The Supreme Court of Canada as National School Board: The Charter and Educational Reform," in Terri Sussel and Michael Manley-Casimir, eds., *Courts in the Classroom: Education and the Charter of Rights and Freedoms* (Calgary: Detselig Enterprises Limited, 1986), at 213.

20. Proceeding with a case through to the Supreme Court of Canada can take over five years and can easily cost in excess of $100,000.

21. For a thorough discussion of the constitutional right to education, see A. Wayne MacKay and Gordon Krinke, "Education as a Basic Human Right: A Response to Special Education and the Charter," *Canadian Journal of Law and Society* (1987), vol. 2, 73.

22. *R. v. Jones*, [1986] 2 S.C.R. 284.

23. Ibid., at 318.

24. *R. v. Oakes* (1986), 26 D.L.R. (4th) 200 (S.C.C.).

25. Ibid., at 277.

26. Ibid., at 224.

27. See A.Wayne MacKay and Lyle I. Sutherland, "Making and Enforcing School Rules in the Wake of the Charter of Rights," in Y.L. Jack Lam, ed., *Canadian Public Education System: Issues and Prospects* (Calgary: Detselig Enterprises Limited, 1990), chapter 4, at 67; see also *Ontario Film and Video Appreciation Society v. Ontario Board of Censors* (1983), 147 D.L.R. (3d) 58 (Ont. Div. Ct.), aff'd (1984), 5 D.L.R. (4th) 766 (Ont. C.A.).

28. See *Southam Inc. v. Hunter* (1984), 55 N.R. 241, at 254 (S.C.C.).

29. The Ontario Court of Appeal has held that principals are permitted to search students under section 8 of the Charter (see *R. v. J.M.G.* (1986), 54 C.R. (3d) 380 (Ont. C.A.)). However, the extent and scope of this power is not yet clear.

30. Outside the Charter context, the Crown generally enjoys immunity from injunctions; however, this immunity is superseded by the powers granted by section 24(1) of the Charter. Dale Gibson, *The Law of the Charter: General Principles* (Toronto: Carswell, 1986), at 210.

31. See, for example, *Re: Hardie and the District of Summerland* (1985), 24 D.L.R. (4th) 257 (B.C.S.C.); see also *Marchand v. Simcoe County Board of Education et al.* (1986), 55 O.R. (2d) 638 (H.C.J.). This power to expand remedial jurisdiction extends only to the superior courts of the provinces that have inherent powers.

32. See *Attorney General for Manitoba v. Metropolitan Stores Ltd. et al.*, [1987] 3 W.W.R. 1 (S.C.C.).

33. See R.J. Sharp, *Injunctions and Specific Performance* (Toronto: Canada Law Book, 1983), at 77.

34. *Tuli v. St. Albert Protestant Board of Education*, unreported decision, April 19, 1985 (Alta. Q.B.); Human Rights Board of Inquiry (December 23, 1986).

35. For a more thorough discussion see *School Law Commentary*, (February 1987), vol. I, issue 6.

36. *Elwood v. Halifax County-Bedford District School Board*, unreported decision, October 1986 (N.S.S.C.T.D.).

37. *Zylberberg*, supra endnote 4.

38. *Corporation of the Canadian Civil Liberties Association et al. v. Ontario (Minister of Education) and Board of Education of Elgin County* (1990), 37 O.A.C. 93.

39. See endnote 34, supra.

40. *Pandori et al. v. The Peel Board of Education* (1990), *School Law Commentary*, Case File No. 5-1-1 (Ont. Human Rights Bd. of Inquiry).

41. (April 26, 1991), *School Law Commentary*, Case File No. 6-1-1 (Ont. H.C.J.).

42. *Kingston v. Board of Trustees Central Okanagan*, unreported decision, November 22, 1984 (B.C.S.C.).

43. *Tinker v. DesMoines Independent Community School District*, 21 L.Ed. 2d 733 (U.S.S.C. 1969).

44. (1988), *School Law Commentary*, Case File No. 3-5-12 (Ont. Div. Ct.).

45. *R. v. Burko* (1968), 3 D.L.R. (3d) 330 (Ont. Mag. Ct.)

46. *Federation of Students of the University of Moncton v. University of Moncton*, unreported decision, December 22, 1982 (N.B.Q.B).

47. *R. v. Kind* (1984), 149 A.P.R. 332 (Nfld. D.C.).

48. *Dolmage v. Muskoka Board of Education* (1985), 49 O.R. (2d) 546 (H.C.J.).

49. *Bales v. Board of School Trustees (Okanagan)* (1984), 8 Adm. L.R. 202 (B.C.S.C.).

50. *Yarmaloy v. Banff School District No. 102* (1985), 16 Adm. L.R. 147 (Alta. Q.B.).

51. Supra endnote 36.

52. *Andrews v. Law Society of British Columbia* [1989], 1 S.C.R. 284.

53. *Carriere v. Lamont Co. School Bd.*, unreported decision, August 15, 1978 (Alta. Q.B.).

54. *Dore v. La Comm. Scholaire de Drummondville* (1983), 4 Can. H.R.R. D/1377 (Que. C.A.).

55. MacKay and Krinke, supra endnote 21.

56. W. MacKay, "Case Comment: *Bales v. Bd. of School Trustees*: Parents, School Boards and Reasonable Special Education" (1985), 8 Adm. L.R. 225.

57. *Hickling v. Lanark-Leeds Roman Catholic School Bd.*, Ontario Board of Inquiry under the Human Rights Code (1986) (Professor B. Adell).

58. *Lanark, Leeds Roman Catholic Separate School Board v. Ontario Human Rights Comm.* (April 1989 Ont. C.A.), summarized in (1989), *School Law Commentary*, vol. 4, no. 1.

59. *Rowett v. The Bd. of Education for York*, unreported decision of the Central Region Special Education Tribunal (1986).

60. *Rowett v. Bd. of Education for York*, unreported decision, June 1, 1989 (Ont. C.A.).

61. Supra endnote 36. A detailed account of this case is presented in J. Batten, *On Trial* (Toronto: MacMillan of Canada, 1988).

62. Unreported decision, October, 1986 (N.S.S.C.T.D.), interlocutory injunction.

63. W. MacKay, "The Elwood Case: Vindicating the Educational Rights of the Disabled," in *Canadian Journal of Special Education* (1987), vol. 3, at 103.

64. Unreported decision, April 28, 1989 (N.B.C.A.), summarized in (1989), *School Law Commentary*, vol. 4, no. 2.

65. In *Elwood v. Halifax County-Bedford District School Board* (1987), the parents of a mentally handicapped child in Nova Scotia were successful in having him integrated into a mainstream classroom two weeks prior to the beginning of the trial. There is no question that the pending legal proceedings were the impetus for the school board to accommodate the parent's requests. See G. Dickinson and A.W. MacKay, *Rights, Freedoms and the Education System in Canada* (Toronto: Emond Montgomery, 1989), 276-85.

66. W. Nightingale, "Teachers Are Not Obliged To Administer Medication to Students," in *N.B.T.A. News* (1985), vol. 27, at 7.

67. W. MacKay, "The Charter of Rights and Special Education: Blessing or a Curse?" in *Canadian Journal for Exceptional Children* (1987), vol. 3, at 118-27.

68. In the United States educationally related medical services have been defined by statutes and judges. *Irving v. Tatro*, 104 S. Ct. 3371 (1984).

69. *Blainey and the Ontario Hockey Association et al.*, (1986), 26 D.L.R. (4th) 728 (Ont. CA).

70. *Halifax Chronicle Herald*, Saturday, October 19, 1991, at 1.

71. *Winnipeg School Division No. 1 v. McCarthur*, [1982] 3 W.W.R. 342 (Man. Q.B.).

72. *R. v. Oakes* (1985), 24 C.C.C. (3d) 321 (S.C.C.).

73. *Ontario Film and Video Appreciation Society v. Ontario Board of Censors* (1984), 5 D.L.R. (4th) 76 (Ont. C.A.). This case insisted that a policy manual be written and made public before it could be used as a section 1 justification.

74. *Re M.B.* (1984), 65 N.S.R. (2d) 181 (N.S. Fam. Ct.).

75. *Mazerolle v. Keith Coughlan and Le District Scholaire* (1987), 83 N.B.R. (2d) 389 (N.B.C.A.).

76. *Re Peel Board of Education et al.* (1987), 59 O.R. (2d) 654 (H.C.J.).

77. *Ingraham v. Wright*, 430 U.S. 651 (1977).

78. *R. v. Ogg-Moss* (1984), 11 D.L.R. (4th) 565 (S.C.C.).

79. *R. v. B.M.*, unreported decision, March 19, 1985 (N.S. Fam. Ct.).

80. See *Peter W. v. San Francisco Unified School District*, 60 Cal. App. (3d) 131 (1976); *Donohue v. Copiague Union Free School District*, 407 N.Y.S. (2d) 874 (1978); *Hoffman v. Board of Education of City of New York*, 424 N.Y.S. (2d) 376 (1979).

81. *Hoffman v. Board of Education of New York*, 410 N.Y.S. (2d) 79 (App. Div. 1978) .

82. *Snow v. State of New York*, 469 N.Y.S. (2d) 959 (1983).

83. *Hicks et al. v. The Board of Education for the City of Etobicoke and the Durham Board of Education* (1988), *School Law Commentary*, Case File No. 3-8-3 (Ont. Dist. Ct.).

84. For a more thorough review of the history and development of copyright law, the reader is directed to chapter 8 of MacKay, supra endnote 13; P. Burnes, *Copyright and Trademark Law in Canada* (Toronto: Coles Publishing, 1978); G. R. Barrel, *Teachers and the Law* (London: Methuen, 1978), 394-419. For a good review of the more recent legislative developments in copyright law, see Diane R. Gagnon, "Copyright in Schools," paper presented to the National C.A.P.S.L.E. Conference in Vancouver, British Columbia, April 29 to May 2, 1990.

85. The Copyright Act, R.S.C. 1985, c. C-42.

86. "Private study" means study by the individual person making the copy and must be bona fide: *University of London Press Ltd. v. University Tutorial Press Ltd.*, [1916] 2 Ch. 6; *Universal City Studios v. Sony Corp. of America*, 104 S. Ct. 774 (1984).

87. For a good description of the various means of copyright enforcement see Anthony R. Lambert, "Enforcement of Copyright," in *Protecting Creative Effort Through Copyright* (Mississauga: Insight Press, 1989).

88. Diane R. Gagnon, "Collective Ownership and Use of Copyright," in *Protecting Creative Effort Through Copyright*, ibid.

3

Teachers as State Agents for the Police

Throughout the discussion of school rules in the previous chapter, there was a conspicuous absence of discussion about how teachers should handle students when there are potential criminal consequences. The reason for this distinction is that the passage of the Young Offenders Act (Y.O.A.) in 1984 has significantly altered the position of school teachers and administrators with respect to young people. The new provisions of the Y.O.A. make it necessary for teachers to delineate between enforcing school rules as an educational state agent and enforcing the criminal law as a police state agent. With the renewed emphasis of provincial governments and school boards on special education and trying to keep children in school through creative truancy programs, teachers are faced with the "unwilling child." In recent times, the children in a mainstream classroom were generally children who wanted to be there. The Y.O.A. combined with a new school board policy of inclusion has created an increasingly difficult classroom situation.

In addition to some of the specific provisions of the Y.O.A., there are a number of Charter concerns that teachers must be aware of as police state agents. In this chapter we will examine the provisions of the Y.O.A. and some of the sections of the Charter that affect the teacher's new role as a state agent for the police.

The Y.O.A. represents a drastic change in the philosophy of juvenile justice in Canada. The previous rehabilitative emphasis of the Juvenile Delinquents Act (J.D.A.) has been replaced by a model that holds young people to be responsible for their actions and, concurrently, recognizes the special guarantees of the rights and freedoms of young people. This new model of juvenile justice should have a significant impact on the manner in which the school system handles young offenders both in the investigation of offences and in the post-disposition treatment of offenders.

The Juvenile Delinquents Act

The Juvenile Delinquents Act of 1908 represented the first codification of a national system of juvenile justice in Canada; however, it may also be viewed as the product of a larger "child saving" movement[1] that had its origins in the late nineteenth century. This movement of social reform was a response to the plight of children brought about by the increasingly urban and industrialized society of the nineteenth and early twentieth centuries.[2] The critical issue for the proponents of this early legislation was not whether a child should be held accountable for his or her behaviour — criminal or otherwise — but rather how best to treat the child so that he or she could become a productive member of society.[3]

These "child saving" origins of delinquency legislation are significant because they represent one of two opposing tensions at play when young people are involved in criminal activity — that is, whether the primary focus should be the protection of children from the harshness of society, or the protection of society from children. This tension has been a recurring theme throughout the development of juvenile justice and continues to haunt the courts under the Y.O.A. In strict legal terms, the doctrine of *parens patriae* provides the basis for state protection "over various classes of persons who, from their legal disability, stand in need of protection, such as infants ... ,"[4] and the federal government's constitutional authority to enact criminal law,[5] which provides the basis for the general protection of society. The original drafting of the J.D.A. in 1908 was the first attempt to balance simultaneously the promotion of child welfare with the perceived need to prevent and control the misbehaviour of children in a criminal context.

The Young Offenders Act

With the exception of a few minor amendments in the 1930s,[6] the J.D.A. remained unchanged until the mid-1960s. However, in 1960, the federal Department of Justice set up a five-member committee to recommend improvements to the juvenile system, and this report, released in 1966, served as the blueprint for the eventual enactment of the Y.O.A. 16 years later.[7] An extensive consultation process took place over the 16-year period between the 1966 report and the final draft of the Y.O.A.; this process included draft legislation and political party proposals.[8]

These proposals addressed the areas that had been identified as problematic under the J.D.A. — that is, the lack of emphasis on

children taking responsibility for their actions, the vagueness of
children's civil rights, the growing public hostility toward serious
and violent young offenders, the age for criminal responsibility, and
the disillusionment with rehabilitative treatment.[9] Perhaps the most
significant problem facing the reformers in the 1970s was the fact
that there had never been a concrete approach to the J.D.A.
developed by either the judiciary or the legal profession, throughout
the history of its operation.[10] This lack of direction may be attributed
to the ambivalence toward lawyers and criminal procedure demon-
strated by the original drafters of the J.D.A.[11] In any event, the task
facing the drafters of the Y.O.A. was to find a "middle ground"
between a paternalistic approach based on rehabilitation and treatment, and the harshness of the adult criminal system.

Application of Code/ Statement of Principle

The Y.O.A. does away with the single charge of delinquency and
replaces it with specific summary conviction and indictable offences
in the Criminal Code. It applies to other federal statutory offences as
well; however, it does not apply to provincial or municipal offences.
The perceived need for individual responsibility as well as the
recognition of civil rights is contained in the "Declaration of Principle" (section 3):

> 3.(1) It is hereby recognized and declared that
> (a) while young persons should not in all instances be held
> accountable in the same manner or suffer the same consequences
> as adults, young persons who commit offences should nonetheless
> bear responsibility for their contraventions; ...
> (e) young persons have rights and freedoms in their own right,
> including those stated in the *Canadian Charter of Rights and
> Freedoms* or in the *Canadian Bill of Rights*, and in particular a right
> to be heard in the course of, and to participate in, the processes
> that lead to decisions that affect them, and young persons should
> have special guarantees of their rights and freedoms;
> (f) in the application of this Act, the rights and freedoms of young
> persons include a right to the least possible interference with
> freedom that is consistent with the protection of society, having
> regard to the needs of young persons and the interests of their
> families; ...

Although these principles appear contradictory, they have been
interpreted as "competing" rather than "inconsistent," and should be
carefully balanced and applied to each fact situation. "Don't apply
the principles uniformly to the hardened 17-year-old and the disad-

vantaged 12-year-old."[12] These principles are, in many ways, the cornerstone of the Y.O.A. because they address the desire to hold children accountable for their actions while making it abundantly clear that the informality prevalent in many provinces under the J.D.A. will not be tolerated under this new scheme.[13]

Age Limitation

Section 2(1) of the Y.O.A. raises the age of criminal responsibility from 7 to 12 years, and the Act applies to persons up to 18 years of age. The effect is to add 16- and 17-year-olds to the provincial juvenile court process. With the exception of truancy legislation, all provinces have enacted statutes to implement the same minimum age restriction for provincial offences.

Alternative Measures

Before the enactment of the Y.O.A., there had been a great deal of debate, both in the United States and in Canada, over the efficacy and scope of "diversion programs."[14] These programs are now termed "alternative measures" under section 4 of the Y.O.A. These alternative measures provide an option, where the young person accepts responsibility for the offence, for the Crown to impose a penalty (for example, an essay on shoplifting) without putting the child through the court system. These measures are usually available only on the young person's first offence, and do not result in any form of criminal record.

A number of problems have arisen in the implementation of alternative measures. First, section 4(1)(a) leaves the structure of these programs in the hands of the provinces, as well as their costs. Nova Scotia has attempted to resolve the cost problem by relying heavily on a volunteer network;[15] however, Ontario simply refused to implement alternative measures. This decision was held to violate section 15 of the Charter of Rights by the Ontario Court of Appeal.[16] This decision was reversed by the Supreme Court of Canada, which concluded that the exercise of governmental discretion was not "law" within the meaning of section 15 of the Charter.[17] A further problem has arisen over whether or not a young person is entitled to notice and to be represented by counsel when the authorities are considering alternative measures. At present, there is no consensus in the courts on this issue;[18] however, there is a strong argument based on section 11(1) of the Act that a young person is entitled to retain and instruct counsel during "any consideration of whether ... to use alternative measures to deal with him."[19]

Detention

The detention of young persons is spelled out in detail under sections 20(1)(k) and 24 of the Y.O.A. A young person cannot be held in custody for a period exceeding two years except in cases where the maximum penalty under the Criminal Code is life, which then may subject the young person to three years' detention. Although the courts determine whether this custody should be "open" or "secure" custody, the province determines the actual placement of any particular offender. This placement cannot, however, be in an adult detention facility, or in a separate wing of an adult detention facility.[20] Before a young person may be committed to custody, the court must consider a pre-disposition report prepared by a youth court worker (section 24(2)), and a failure to do this renders the committal to custody a nullity.[21] Teachers can certainly be helpful in the preparation of a pre-disposition report. As part of the report, the court will want to know whether the particular offender can function in a mainstream school environment, or whether custody is a more suitable option.

Detention Prior to Disposition

Young persons may also be detained prior to disposition through section 7 of the Y.O.A., although there are provisions that allow them to be released into the care of a responsible person (section 7.1). To be successful in obtaining a custody order before trial or sentencing, the Crown must establish that detention is necessary to ensure the accused's attendance in court, or to ensure the protection and safety of the public.

The system of interim detention is open to abuse with some young offenders in cases where there is an overlap with child welfare legislation. In the case of *R. v. D.B.*,[22] a 14-year-old offender convicted of two relatively minor theft-related offences was remanded into custody for 10 days prior to sentencing. He had run away from an abusive home and, consequently, had no place to live. The representatives from social services admitted in court that D.B. was a "child in need of protection" but refused to apprehend him because they could not find an available placement. The Crown argued that because the young person had no parental supervision, detention was necessary to ensure his attendance in court. A successful *habeas corpus* application was made to the Nova Scotia Supreme Court[23] and the young person was moved from detention to a designated place of safety. This illustrates the need to sometimes balance the Criminal Code provisions with the special circumstances of young offenders.

Right to Counsel

Section 11 of the Y.O.A. is a clear indication of the shift toward due process and the new emphasis on civil rights for young people because it gives young offenders the right to retain and instruct counsel without delay at any stage of the proceedings, and enables the offender to exercise this right personally. When the Y.O.A. was first enacted, it was silent on the personal exercise of this right, and the Manitoba Court of Appeal held that a young person did not have the capacity to retain and instruct counsel.[24] The Act was consequently amended to allow young people to retain counsel directly. Section 11(2) requires that every young person who is arrested or detained shall be informed of his right to retain and instruct counsel forthwith. This is stronger wording than that of section 10(b) of the Charter of Rights, which requires the opportunity for adults to retain and instruct counsel "without delay." Section 11 of the Y.O.A. therefore places a strict requirement on arresting officers.

Sentencing

Under section 20 of the Y.O.A., judges have a wide range of sentencing options. These include absolute discharge, fines, restitution, community service hours, treatment orders, and probation. One of the primary similarities between the J.D.A. and the Y.O.A. is the reliance on probation as a means of correction. Under section 20(1)(j), a youth court may make a probation order containing terms and conditions pursuant to section 23 of the Act, including "such other reasonable conditions set out in the order as the court considers desirable" (section 23(2)(g)). The difference between probation under the Y.O.A. and the J.D.A. is that judges must now be careful to spell out clearly the terms and conditions of probation. In *R. v. P.D.F.*,[25] a probation order was held to be too vague to be enforceable under section 26 of the Y.O.A. because it simply required the youth to "live with mother and obey rules and curfew." Judge Naismith further held that, if these terms were "fleshed out" by someone else by way of delegation (for example, a youth court worker), it would amount to an unlawful delegation of a judicial function and consequently be invalid.

The School: Investigative Role

Often, children who experience difficulty with authority structures in the school setting experience the same difficulty with the authority structures of criminal law. For this reason, it is important that education professionals appreciate the implications of the Y.O.A. and be familiar with its basic operation. Previously, school officials relied on ad hoc and informal procedures when they investigated offences committed by students, and were loath to involve any formal legal figures. The lack of criminal procedure under the J.D.A. provided the luxury of involving "the law" at any time during the investigative process. The Y.O.A. has ushered in a new era in which special safeguards must be adhered to from the outset of any investigation of a young offender.

Section 24(2) of the Charter of Rights provides that any evidence obtained in a manner that violates an individual's rights may be excluded, if to admit the evidence would bring the administration of justice into disrepute. Under section 3(e) of the Y.O.A., young people have a "special guarantee" of this evidentiary protection; therefore, authorities must be particularly careful when dealing with young offenders. School officials may well be barred from pursuing a criminal prosecution in cases where informal searches or questioning procedures violate the protections afforded to young people, and, consequently, result in evidence being excluded.

Arrest and Detention

Educators have the capacity to act both as educational state agents and as agents of the police and, as mentioned earlier, it is not always clear in any given situation which role is being assumed.[26] Section 10 of the Charter of Rights requires police "on arrest or detention" to inform the accused promptly of the reasons for arrest, to inform the accused of his or her right to retain and instruct counsel, and to provide the opportunity to retain and instruct counsel without delay. Section 11(2) of the Y.O.A. requires the young person to be advised of his or her right to counsel "forthwith" upon arrest or detention by the arresting officer. If an educator who is acting as an agent of the police detains a young person for questioning he or she may be required to comply with the requirements of section 10(b) of the Charter and section 11 of the Y.O.A.

In R. v. J.M.G.,[27] the Ontario Court of Appeal examined a situation in which a principal detained a young person in order to conduct a search for narcotics. Justice Grange assumed that the principal was acting in an educational capacity; however, he was not clear on whether a principal should ever adhere to the section 10(b) Charter requirement, other than to concede that in "serious" cases a principal should either comply with the Charter or involve the police. Justice Grange further clouded the issue by claiming that students are in a "constant state of detention" while in school and, therefore, it is impossible for them to be detained within the meaning of section 10 of the Charter. This likens the school setting to a prison[28] and clearly violates the established principle in the United States that students do not shed their constitutional rights at the schoolhouse gates.[29] The approach of Justice Grange is also unacceptable in that it does not adequately protect the individual rights of the student who faces the same consequences whether the investigation is conducted by the principal or the police.

A better approach was outlined by Provincial Court Judge Michel in the case of *R. v. L.L.*,[30] where a young person was questioned for an hour and a half about a stolen sum of money. At the outset, it had been made clear that no criminal consequences would follow; however, when the student admitted to having purchased narcotics with the money and the marijuana was found in his possession, the police were called. At the Provincial Court level, Judge Michel excluded the relevant evidence because of the violation of the student's constitutional rights.

Judge Michel found that there should be a clear line between the educating and policing roles of educators, and suggested that different rules apply when the detention is used to enforce a strictly in-house rule, or a criminal violation. In the former case, the teacher or principal is acting as an educational agent and need not be concerned with reading a student his or her Charter rights or involving legal counsel. If the breach of the school rule could also lead to criminal charges, regardless of their "seriousness," then, he concluded, a student is entitled to his or her Charter rights whether the investigation is conducted by the police or the school authorities.

The decision of Judge Michel was reversed at the District Court level.[31] That court found that there was no detention because there was no original intention to involve criminal authorities and, in any event, the judge held that the youth had consented to the detention. The idea of voluntariness is dubious whenever a student is confronted by school authorities, and, surely, L.L. consented on the basis that there would be no criminal consequences.

The question of how best to detain a child for investigation while maintaining the integrity of his or her Charter protections still remains. Clearly, the courts are yielding to the discretion of educators in these situations, even though this is inconsistent with the special protections afforded to young offenders under section 3(e) of the Y.O.A. Most educators welcome this discretion because they are not prepared to inform children of their "rights" upon every detention. We would recommend, however, that school officials take a proactive stance in this area and set guidelines that are consistent with the Y.O.A. protections. If the purpose of the detention is to enforce an in-house rule, no warnings or legal counsel are required. However, if criminal proceedings are contemplated, the young person should be informed about the nature of the allegation, and at least be permitted to contact a parent before any further investigation takes place. It is necessary to maintain order and discipline, but schools also serve as a microcosm of society at large. There is, therefore, an educational as well as a legal basis for offering the protections guaranteed by the Charter of Rights.

Search and Seizure

Section 8 of the Charter of Rights guarantees individuals the right to be free from unreasonable search and seizure:

> s. 8 Everyone has the right to be secure against unreasonable search and seizure.

In the case of *Hunter v. Southam*,[32] Justice Dickson set out four principles governing search and seizure. First he stated that section 8 creates a "right to privacy," or a right "to be let alone."[33] Second, he found searches without a warrant to be *prima facie* unreasonable; there is a presumption against the "searcher" that must be rebutted. Third, he dealt with the general constitutionality of searches:

> An assessment of the constitutionality of a search and seizure ... must focus on its reasonable or unreasonable impact on the subject of the search or seizure, and not simply on its rationality in furthering a valid government objective.[34]

His final principle addressed balancing the need for crime control with the protection of privacy rights, in which he concluded that the balance was achieved at the point where "credibly based probability replaces suspicion."[35] The person conducting the search must, therefore, have some grounds above mere suspicion before engaging in the search.

In the school setting, students will be viewed as having a right "to be let alone" and any search will be deemed unreasonable unless the school official can provide a justification based on the impact of the search on the particular student. This is essentially the same test applied by the U.S. Supreme Court in the leading case of *New Jersey v. T.L.O.*[36] In that case, a 14-year-old girl had her purse searched by the school principal who, while looking for tobacco cigarettes, found marijuana and a list of names implicating T.L.O. as a narcotics dealer. The court held that the constitutional prohibitions against unreasonable search and seizure applied to school officials, but found the search to be constitutionally valid because it was not excessively intrusive in the light of the age of the student, and was therefore reasonable under the circumstances. The standard of "reasonableness" applied by Justice White is one that "would not unduly burden the efforts of school authorities to maintain order, nor would it authorize unrestrained intrusions of privacy."[37]

The standard effectively requires school officials to have a "reasonable suspicion" that their search will turn up evidence, rather than "probable cause" that such evidence will be found.[38] Although this appears to violate the fourth principle set out by Chief Justice Dickson in *Hunter*, the importance of crime control in the school system would lead the courts to apply a similar test in Canada. This appears to be the approach taken by Justice Grange in *R. v. J.M.G.*,[39] Canada's leading case on the issue.

Personal Search

There are three types of searches that commonly occur in the school setting: personal, locker, and blanket or "dragnet" searches. The most frequent, and most contentious, is the personal search. The Ontario Court of Appeal had the opportunity to review a personal search in the school setting in *R. v. J.M.G.*, where a principal searched a student's socks after being informed by another student that J.M.G. was in possession of narcotics. The principal found marijuana and the student was charged with possession. Justice Grange upheld the search as reasonable, although he did not spell out whether the authority to search stemmed from the common law doctrine of *in locus parentis*, or as an implication of the statutory duty to maintain order and discipline. As discussed earlier, the latter is the more realistic analysis and the one that allows the student to call in aid the Charter protections against unreasonable searches.[40]

The *J.M.G.* situation clearly fits into the test from *T.L.O.* because the principal had a reasonable suspicion and the search was not excessively intrusive. There are, however, situations that may arise that would not be so easily dealt with. First, there is the case where a student is being searched for breach of a school rule (for example, smoking in the bathroom) and, in the course of the investigation, the school official discovers grounds for a criminal charge (marijuana). Should the evidence be admissible? In *T.L.O.*, the evidence was admissible under this fact situation because the court failed to delineate between a suspected breach of a school rule and the suspected breach of criminal law. The appropriate solution would be to admit evidence obtained through a bona fide search for breach of a school rule, but exclude evidence where the school official has engaged in a "fishing expedition," or where a search was not reasonably necessary to establish that a school rule had been broken.

There is further potential for trouble in cases where the student does not cooperate in the search, or even physically resists. What are the limits on the extent of the search? In *R. v. Morrison*,[41] the Ontario Court of Appeal upheld a strip search of an adult woman charged with theft and possession of stolen property; however, the search was conducted at the police station in the presence of a female officer and was incidental to a lawful arrest. Unless there is some element of imminent danger or urgency, it does not seem appropriate for school personnel to strip search young offenders. Further, if the student physically resists the search, the police should be called. A principal certainly has a responsibility to maintain discipline and order in his or her school, but crime control is the job of law enforcement agencies and should be left in their hands whenever this is reasonably practicable.

Locker Search

The second common type of search in schools is the locker search. Although there is some debate over the right of students to "exclusive possession" of their lockers,[42] it is unrealistic to expect the courts to declare lockers "out of bounds" for school personnel. The crux of the problem is that lockers create an expectation of privacy among students, and some consideration ought to be given to this expectation.[43] In the United States, students have been held to have exclusive possession of lockers vis-à-vis other students, but not to have such exclusivity over the locker as against school authorities.[44] The simple course of actions for schools, then, is to dispel any notion of privacy by notifying students at the beginning of each school year that their lockers are school property and may be subject to search at any time.[45]

Dragnet Searches

The third type of search involves searching a large group of children in order to discover one or two offenders; it is commonly referred to as a "blanket" or "dragnet" search. In the U.S. case of *Bellnier v. Lund*,[46] for example, an entire fifth grade class was strip searched in order to find an individual who had stolen three dollars. This search was ruled "unreasonable" by the courts. In another U.S. decision, *Jones et al. v. Latexo Independent School District*,[47] the court reinstated two suspended students and held that "the blanket search or dragnet is, except in the most unusual and compelling circumstances, anathema to the protection accorded citizens under the

Fourth Amendment."[48] The Canadian courts have dealt with a similar situation in the case of *R. v. Heisler*.[49] This case involved a random search at a rock concert in order to isolate a few offenders. Random searches are indistinguishable from blanket searches because both involve searching a large number of people without probable cause. The Alberta Provincial Court struck down this type of search as unconstitutional because the defendant should have been given the option of consenting to the search or leaving the concert. This indicates that the courts are likely to be sympathetic toward the position taken in the United States on blanket searches.

Questioning and Admissibility of Statements

Persons in Authority

The use of questioning is widespread in Canadian schools and can act as a powerful tool in gathering evidence against young offenders. Educators have previously enjoyed a good deal of latitude in this area; however, the Y.O.A. will serve to restrict this latitude. Section 56 sets the ground rules that must be met before statements can be admitted as evidence. The first important feature of this section is that it applies to "persons in authority." In *Rothman v. The Queen*,[50] the Supreme Court of Canada defined the statutory interpretation of "persons in authority" to be a subjective test; therefore, if teachers are regarded as persons in authority by their students, they will be similarly regarded by the law. "Authority" is not used in the colloquial sense, but must involve a belief by the accused that the person can influence the course of prosecution.[51] In *R. v. H.*,[52] both the youth court and the Alberta Queen's Bench agreed that teachers are persons in authority for the purposes of section 56(2). It is reasonable to expect courts across Canada to reach the same conclusion.

Given that school officials will be considered persons in authority, they will have to be aware of the requirements under section 56(2), if they wish to use statements given by a student in criminal proceedings. The first criterion, under paragraph (a), is that the statement be "voluntary." This term has a long and complicated legal history; however, it is sufficient for the purposes of this discussion to treat this as meaning that statements must be given "without fear of prejudice or hope of advantage exercised or held out by a person in authority."[53] In the school setting, then, threats of after-school detentions or promises that "things will go easier if you just tell the truth" may render statements inadmissible.

Informing Youths of Their Rights

The second criterion, set out in section 56(2)(b), is more problematic because it forces educators to act as police officers in "reading a student her rights." Unlike the debate over informing students of their right to instruct counsel upon detention, the Y.O.A. is clear that a student must be informed of his or her rights under paragraph (b) if his or her statement is to be used as evidence against the student. This is an area that relates directly to the change in philosophy from the J.D.A. because it emphasizes the need to protect the rights of children at every stage of the criminal process. It is important to note that the student is to have these rights explained in a language that he or she understands. U.S. studies have shown that children do not fully understand or appreciate their rights when given in a U.S. "Miranda-type" warning.[54] It is, therefore, advisable for school boards to draft a proper format for advising students of their rights, to be used in schools. Perhaps instituting a policy of no questioning in cases where clear criminal consequences are involved would be even more appropriate. Questioning is properly a matter for the police.

The final significant impact of section 56 lies in paragraph (c). This paragraph allows a youth to consult with a parent, counsel, relative, or "other appropriate adult" before making a statement. This raises the general difficulty and time-consuming effort involved in contacting one of those individuals; however, if the student has been detained, there should already have been an attempt made to contact an appropriate adult.

A specific problem arises when the student chooses a teacher to be the "other appropriate adult." A recent amendment to the Y.O.A. sets out that persons consulted under section 56(2)(c) are not persons in authority for the purposes of this section.[55] Statements made to a teacher acting in this capacity may therefore be admissible against the accused without the protections included in section 56(2)(b). Teachers should be particularly careful when asked to consult a young person so that they are not put in the awkward position of betraying the confidence of the accused. If the Crown subpoenaed the teacher to testify at the trial of the student, the teacher would be required, by law, to relate all of the conversation that the student obviously thought was held in confidence. If a lawyer is consulted pursuant to paragraph (c), the conversation is protected by solicitor-client privilege. This privilege does not extend to teachers. We suggest that teachers not act as advisers under this paragraph in cases where there is a potential for serious criminal consequences.[56]

The area of questioning students brings the importance of delineating between criminal and in-house investigations into sharper perspective. Section 56 leaves little room for discretion on the part of educators; it comes into operation immediately if any of the statements given by the accused are to be used as evidence against him or her.[57] The Supreme Court of Canada has determined that the requirements of section 56 are to be strictly adhered to no matter how old or "street-wise" a child may appear.[58] This reinforces the argument presented earlier that educators should develop different procedures when handling young offenders than normally practised when enforcing school rules. In fact, we suggest that the difficulties of both questioning and searching students make it advisable to develop a closer relationship with police officers and to use the resources of the police force to deal with situations involving criminal activity.

Arrest

Because the minimum age of criminal responsibility is 12 years, the impact of the Y.O.A. for elementary school teachers (that is, up to grade 6) and principals is only relevant when conducting investigations of criminal activity committed by young people outside the realm of the elementary school context. There may be cases, for example, of children from a nearby high school vandalizing school property, or selling drugs to younger children. In these instances, the elementary school official should take positive action to stop the activity in question.

For the most part, consideration should be given to the issues of searching and questioning discussed earlier, because the same rules will apply to an elementary school teacher dealing with a young offender. The primary difference will occur in the detention of the accused; a high school student may not "voluntarily" submit to being detained in an elementary school. In cases where an offender will not cooperate with school authorities, it is possible to make a "citizen's arrest." Section 494 of the Criminal Code allows citizens to make arrests when they find someone committing an indictable offence, or when the citizen believes the individual is being "freshly pursued" by the police.

Indictable offences are generally serious offences such as theft over $1,000 (section 334(a)), robbery (theft with violence or threat of violence; section 343), sexual assault (section 271(1)), assault (section 266), vandalism (mischief; section 430), and the possession or trafficking of illicit drugs (section 3 and section 4 of the Narcotics

Control Act.[59] If an elementary school official witnesses one of these or similar offences, he or she has the lawful authority to place the accused under arrest, and deliver him or her to the police as soon as reasonably practicable. Because arrest is a highly intrusive act, a citizen should be cautious in exercising this power. There is the further danger of civil liability for false imprisonment in cases where a citizen arrests without lawful authority. For example, if a teacher was simply told about an offence and did not actually witness the event, there would be no power to arrest under section 494 of the Criminal Code.

An arrest is effected by the uttering of words indicating that the person is under arrest and touching the person with a view to detention.[60] Once the person has been detained, he or she should be informed of the reasons for the arrest, and the person's right to retain and instruct counsel (or a parent) without delay, and be given access to a telephone. The requirements under section 494(3) state that the arrested person must be delivered to a police officer "forthwith"; therefore, there will ordinarily be no time for questioning. If, however, the young person is questioned, he or she should be informed of their rights under section 56 of the Y.O.A.

Student Records and the Young Offenders Act

An additional issue with regard to young offenders is the relationship between the duty to maintain a student record and section 38 of the Y.O.A., which prohibits the publication of the identity of a young offender. On a strict reading of section 38, it is unlawful for teachers to note on the student record whether the student has been charged or convicted with an offence under the Y.O.A. because this would effectively "publish" the name of the offender.

This is a distressing development for two reasons. First, in cases where a student has been subject to custody as a result of his or her offence and, therefore, was absent from school for three or four months in a given grade, it may be absolutely vital for the future instruction of this pupil to have this absence noted in the student's record. In the next chapter, we will discuss in more detail the school's role as a rehabilitative agency for young offenders after their custodial disposition. The second distressing reason is that most teachers would certainly like to know whether or not they have a potentially violent child in their classroom — particularly in cases where the child has transferred school jurisdictions or even provinces and his school record contains no reference to a violent crime in his past (for example, sexual assault). In Ontario, the regulations specifically restrict the identification of any offences in the student record; however, it is arguable that whether or not there is a regulation in place to that effect, section 38 of the Y.O.A. is paramount and will prevail over all provincial legislation.

Perhaps an argument can be made that the restricted access to student records is sufficient protection for the young person so that the notation of a criminal offence in the record is, therefore, not "publication." In one Ontario case, however, the Supreme Court determined that a school board could not hold an expulsion hearing because the hearing would inevitably lead to the publication of the identities of the accused through their absence at school. Given this broad definition of "publication," it will be difficult for the courts to allow the notation of offences in the student record in the face of section 38 of the Y.O.A.

You Be the Judge — A Scenario

Having now looked at enforcing rules under the Charter in a school context and enforcing the Criminal Code as a police state agent under the Y.O.A., we offer the following scenario for consideration as an exercise to examine some of the difficult issues teachers and administrators may face with the Y.O.A. This scenario has arisen from two cases in which schools have taken disciplinary actions (that is, through in-house school rule mechanisms) against students charged, but not yet convicted, under the Y.O.A. It illustrates a classic dilemma between protecting a young person's Charter rights and maintaining a safe and orderly environment in the school. There is no clear, correct course of action that will reconcile all of the interests involved in these cases.

The first case[61] arose in a Saskatchewan school where three students had been charged, but pleaded "not guilty" to allegations of sexual assault. In response to these charges, the school placed the youths on "short bounds" restrictions, which required them to go immediately to their classroom upon arrival and remain there for the duration of the day except to attend physical education classes, and to move through the halls only with permission of a staff member. The parents challenged these restrictions. However, Justice MacLellan found this to be a valid exercise of the school board's power to "exercise general supervision and control over schools" pursuant to section 91 of the Education Act.[62]

The second case[63] occurred in Ontario, where four youths pleaded not guilty to charges of forcible confinement and sexual assault. They were subsequently suspended by the principal of the school. The Peel Board of Education upheld the suspensions and moved to have the students expelled. They initiated an application to the Ontario Supreme Court to determine whether the proposed expulsion hearing would offend section 38 of the Y.O.A., which prohibits the publication of the identity of a young offender. Justice Reid held that the expulsion hearing could not proceed because it would inevitably lead to the publication of the identities of the accused, as well as prematurely stigmatize the youths as "guilty." Justice Reid went further to state:

> This comes distressingly close to condemnation without trial. The principal seems to have assumed that the students were guilty simply because they were charged. That is wholly contrary to the fundamental principle of our system of justice. Everyone is presumed innocent until found guilty by due process of law. Had the principal not jumped to the conclusion that the students were guilty he would have had no basis for ordering their suspension.[64]

There are two important principles in conflict in both of these cases. The first principle is that school authorities should suspend children who are suspected of criminal conduct so that other students in the school are not put at risk. The second is that everyone has the right to be presumed innocent, and children particularly should not be stigmatized as "guilty" when they may in fact be innocent. Although the Ontario case focuses on protecting the identity of young offenders, the presumption of innocence is arguably the more significant issue in that case.

There are no simple answers to the questions that arise when a student is charged with a serious criminal offence. Section 7 of the Charter protects the rights of children to receive an education and not to be deprived of that right except in accordance with principles of fundamental justice. Furthermore, section 11(d) of the Charter guarantees the presumption of innocence. On the other hand, there are good public policy reasons for limiting these rights where school children are potentially at risk, and section 1 of the Charter allows school authorities to create reasonable limits.

We suggest that placing "short bounds" restrictions on students such as those used by the school in Saskatchewan may be an appropriate compromise, but this is far from definitive. There are a number of variables to be considered in each case — these include the character of the students involved and the seriousness of the offence with which they are charged. Regardless of the manner in which schools deal with a particular case, it is important that school boards develop written policies for implementing discipline procedures so that the procedures can be defended under section 1 of the Charter as limits that are "prescribed by law." School boards should also be sensitive to the need for protecting the identity of young offenders wherever possible.

The meshing of statutes, regulations, and policies was difficult even before the Charter's enactment. The additional challenge of the Charter in the discipline process has sent some educators scurrying for cover. There have, however, been few actual Charter challenges. There is still time for the educators to put their own houses in order, before the courts require them to. Given that the classroom teacher often experiences the frontline contact with many of these students, it is vital that teachers take an active role in this process. A careful in-house review of rules, procedures, and penalties may prevent legal action and give educators a greater sense of being in control of their own destinies. Action is better than reaction.

ENDNOTES

1. For a discussion of the "child-saving" movement in the United States, see Anthony Platt, *The Child Savers: The Invention of Delinquency* (Chicago: University of Chicago Press, 1969); see also Graham Parker, "American Child Saving: The Climate of Reform as Reflected in the National Conference of Charities and Corrections, 1875 – 1900," in *University of Toronto Law Journal* (1968), vol. 18, at 371.

2. G. Parker, "Century of the Child," in *Canadian Bar Review* (1967), vol. 45, at 741. The child-saving movement in Canada was represented by W.L. Scott and J.J. Kelso, who lobbied extensively for delinquency legislation and, consequently, played a major role in drafting the J.D.A. of 1908.

3. Jeffrey Leon, "The Development of Canadian Juvenile Justice: A Background for Reform," in *Osgoode Hall Law Journal* (1977), vol.15, no.1, 71, at 81.

4. *Jowitts Dictionary of English Law.*

5. Constitution Act, 1867, s. 91(27).

6. S.C. 1929, c. 46; 1932, c. 17; 1935, c. 41; 1936, c. 40; 1947, c. 37; 1949 (1st Sess.), c. 6.

7. Department of Justice, *Juvenile Delinquency in Canada: The Report of the Department of Justice Committee on Juvenile Delinquency* (Ottawa: Queen's Printer, 1965).

8. Susan Reid and Marie Reitsma-Street, "Assumptions and Implications of New Canadian Legislation for Young Offenders," in *Canadian Criminal Forum* (1984), vol. 7, no. 1, 1, at 2.

9. Peter Gabor, Ian Greene, and Peter McCormick, "The Young Offenders Act: The Alberta Youth Court Experience in the First Year," in *Canadian Journal of Family Law* (1986), vol. 5, at 301; see also Raymond Corrado, "Juvenile Justice: From Creation and Optimism to Disillusionment and Reform," at 27; Neil Boyd, "The Circularity of Punishment and Treatment: Some Notes on the Legal Response to Juvenile Delinquency," in *Canadian Journal of Family Law* (1980), vol. 3, at 419. Boyd argues convincingly that the major problem with the rehabilitative ideal of juvenile institutions was the contradiction inherent in the goals of custody and treatment.

10. D.M. Steinberg (Judge of Ont. Prov. Ct.), "The Young Offender and the Courts" (1972), 6 R.F.L. 86, at 87.

11. Leon, supra endnote 3, at 94 and 102.

12. *R. v. R.Q.* (1985), Y.O.S. 15.11, Dig. 5 (Ont. Prov. Ct.).

13. Bala and Lilles, *The Young Offenders Act Annotated* (Toronto: Butterworths, 1986), at 14.

14. Julian Rappaport, "Public Policy and the Dilemmas of Diversion," in Raymond Corrado, Marc LeBlanc, and Jean Trépanier, *Current Issues in Juvenile Justice* (Toronto: Butterworths, 1983), at 169.

15. The volunteer network in Nova Scotia is coordinated by the Youth Alternative Society, which is funded by the province.

16. *R. v. Sheldon S.* (1988), 26 O.A.C. 285.

17. *R. v. Sheldon S.* (1990), 110 N.R. 321 (S.C.C.).

18. *R. v. R.Q.*, supra endnote 12, where charges were dismissed because police and the Crown did not consider alternative measures for a young first offender, and did not allow him to retain and instruct counsel before charges were laid; *contra*, see *Re T.W. and the Queen* (1986), 25 C.C.C.(3d) 89 (Sask. Q.B.), where Judge Armstrong held that the decision to lay charges is the historical prerogative of the Crown, and if Parliament had intended to alter it, they would have stated so expressly. In *R. v. J.B.* (1985), 20 C.C.C. (3d) 67 (Ont. Prov. Ct.), Provincial Court Judge Collings compromised by finding that there is no duty to consider alternative measures; however, if such measures are considered, the young person should be given notice and the opportunity to participate.

19. Jeffrey Wilson and Mary Tomlinson, *Children and the Law*, 2d ed. (Toronto: Butterworths, 1986), at 352-53.

20. See the discussion of *Re L.H.F.* (P.E.I.S.C.) and *Re Darren B.* (N.S.S.C.) by Heino Lilles in *Young Offenders Service*, Annotation 15.24.1 Ann. 4.

21. *R. v. M.S.S.* (1985), 23 C.C.C. (3d) 95 (Sask. C.A.), *R. v. J.D.B.*, summarized in 1 W.C.B. (2d) 344 (B.C.C.A.), and *R. v. D.W.H.*, summarized in 17 W.C.B. 180 (Alta. C.A.).

22. *R. v. D.B.*, unreported decision, February 17, 1988, (N.S. Yth. Ct.), per Roscoe Fam. Ct. J.

23. Unreported decision, February 22, 1988, per Kelly J.

24. *R. v. W.W.W.* (1985), 20 C.C.C. (3d) 214 (Man. C.A.).

25. *R. v. P.D.F.* (1987), 57 C.R. (3d) 22 (Ont. Prov. Ct.).

26. A. Wayne MacKay and Lyle I. Sutherland, "Making and Enforcing School Rules in the Wake of the Charter of Rights," in Y.L. Jack Lam, ed., *Canadian Public Education System: Issues and Prospects* (Calgary: Detselig Enterprises, 1990).

27. *R. v. J.M.G.* (1987), 54 C.R. (3d) 380 (Ont. C.A.) (leave to appeal to the Supreme Court of Canada denied).

28. For a more detailed analysis of the "school as prison" analogy see: A. Wayne MacKay, "*R. v. J.M.G.* Case Comment: Students as Second Class Citizens Under the Charter" (1987), 54 C.R. (3d) 390. For an alternative view see Bruce E. Thom, Q.C. and Douglas J. Thom, "School Order and Discipline Preferred Over Students' Rights: R. v. G. (J.M.)," in *Education & Law Journal* (1990-91), vol. 3, at 105.

29. *Tinker v. Des Moines Independent Community School District*, 21 L. Ed. (2d) 733, at 737 (U.S.S.C. 1969).

30. *R. v. L.L.*, unreported decision, June 25, 1985 (Ont. Prov. Ct.). See (1986), *School Law Commentary*, Case File No. 1-3-4.

31. *R. v. L.L.*, unreported decision, April 25, 1986, (Ont. Dist. Ct.).

32. *Hunter v. Southam* (1984), 14 C.C.C. (3d) 97 (S.C.C.).

33. Ibid., at 108.

34. Ibid., at 106.

35. Ibid., at 115.

36. *New Jersey v. T.L.O.*, 83 L. Ed. (2d) 720 (U.S.S.C.). For a critical comment of this decision see Susan M. Mooney, "New Jersey v. T.L.O.: The School Search Exception to Probable Cause," in *New England Law Review*, vol. 21, no. 2, at 509.

37. R.V. Farley, "The Charter and Student Rights," in T. Wuester and E. Nicholls, *Education Law and the Canadian Charter of Rights and Freedoms* (Vancouver: B.C. School Trustees Assoc., 1986), 26, at 32.

38. Lyman Robinson, "The Charter and Searches and Seizures in Schools," in T. Wuester and A. Nicholls, ibid., at 96.

39. *R. v. J.M.G.*, supra endnote 27.

40. "*R. v. J.M.G.* Case Comment," supra endnote 28, at 397.

41. *R. v. Morrison* (1987), 35 C.C.C. (3d) 437 (Ont. C.A.).

42. Robinson, supra endnote 38, at 99.

43. Ibid., at 98.

44. *People v. Overton* (1967), 229 N.E. (2d) 598.

45. This approach was upheld in *Zamora v. Pomeroy*, 639 F.2d 665, where school board regulations provided, inter alia, "1. The school retains jurisdiction over lockers even though lockers are assigned to particular students. 2. The administration may inspect lockers at any time."

46. *Bellnier v. Lund*, 438 F. Supp. 47 (N.D.N.Y. 1977).

47. *Jones et al. v. Latexo Independent School District*, 499 F. Supp. 223 (Dist. Ct. Texas 1980).

48. Robinson, supra endnote 38, at 97.

49. *R. v. Heisler* (1983), 7 C.R.R. 1 (Alta. Prov. Ct.).

50. *Rothman v. The Queen* (1981), 59 C.C.C. (3d) 30 (S.C.C.).

51. *R. v. A.B.* (1986), 50 C.R. (3d) 247, at 258 (Ont. C.A.). See also Nicholas Bala, "Questioning of Young Suspects" (1986), 50 C.R. (3d) 260.

52. *R. v. H.* (1985), 43 Alta. L.R. (2d) 250 (Prov. Ct.). Unreported decision, June 26, 1986 (Alta. Q.B.): see *School Law Commentary*, vol. 1, no. 1.

53. Bala and Lilles, supra endnote 13. See *Ibrahim v. The King*, [1914] A.C. 599, at 609 (P.C.) for this proposition.

54. A.B. Ferguson and A.C. Douglas, "A Study of Juvenile Waiver," in *San Diego Law Review* (1970), vol. 7, no. 1, at 38.

55. 1986, c. 32, s. 38, and s. 56(6).

56. Teachers should also be aware that there is no duty placed on them to act as an adviser; see Lyman Robinson, "The Young Offenders Act," in *Canadian School Executive* (October 1984).

57. In *R. v. H.*, supra endnote 52, four students confessed to having stolen a sum of money from a teacher. They were originally told that there would be no consequences if the money was returned; however, when the principal heard the confessions he called the police and the youths were charged with theft. The confessions were excluded and the youths were consequently acquitted because the

principal had not informed them of their rights pursuant to section 56 of the Y.O.A.

58. *R. v. J.T.* (1990), 59 C.C.C. (3d) 1 (S.C.C.).

59. R.S.C. 1985, c. N-1.

60. *R. v. Whitfield* (1970), 9 C.R.N.S. 59 (S.C.C.).

61. *H. et al. v. Board of Education of the Shamrock School Division No. 38 of Saskatchewan* (1987), 57 Sask. R. 188 (Q.B.).

62. The sole ground relied on by the applicant was that the school board had acted in excess of the powers granted by s. 91 of the Education Act. (See *H. et al.*, supra endnote 61, at 190).

63. *Re Peel Board of Education et al.* (1987), 59 O.R. (2d) 654 (H.C.J.).

64. Ibid., at 661. See also Judith Anderson, "Expulsion Hearing Contrary to Young Offenders Act," in *Canadian School Executive*, vol. 7, no. 4, 23, at 25.

4

Teachers as Social Welfare Agents

This chapter looks at how the teacher functions in the school environment as a social welfare agent. This is one of the more recently emerging roles of teachers necessitated by government's increased involvement in the welfare of children, as seen through more developed children's aid societies and the passage of the Young Offenders Act (Y.O.A.). The role in itself is a complex mixture of a number of different roles and areas of law. We will examine each one of these roles independently and provide a brief description of the elements of each role. This chapter focuses on the identification of the roles rather than on a thorough explanation of each role. In many cases, simply identifying the role is half the battle.

We will begin by examining the teacher as a rehabilitative counsellor for young offenders in the school and then look more generally at the teacher, particularly guidance counsellors, as social workers. We will also look at the responsibilities of teachers as child advocates both internally, within the school, and externally, with agencies outside the school. In that external context, we will look specifically at the teacher's role as a coordinator of these outside agencies. Finally, we will examine some of the family law issues that spill into the school environment and involve teachers as family mediators.

Teacher as Y.O.A. Rehab Counsellor

The unique provisions of the Y.O.A. provide an additional burden on the school system to act in the rehabilitation of young offenders. The scheme of the Y.O.A. provides for both punishment and rehabilitation. The federal government, however, left it to the provinces to fund the actual programs that will implement these goals. As a result, many of the less affluent provinces have not been able to put in place the "cadillac" rehabilitation programs that are seen as desirable for young offenders. The facilities for young offenders are primarily detention facilities that were built in a rush to satisfy the requirements of open-custody detention. As a result, the courts have looked to the school systems to pick up the slack in the area of rehabilitation. It is very tempting for a judge when sentencing a young offender to sentence him or her to a period of probation in which the child has to "attend school and obey all of the rules of school." Unfortunately, judges cannot order (or pay for) the extra resources required by classroom teachers to deal with these children.

Historically, education has been seen as an important tool in the rehabilitation of young offenders. Egerton Ryerson, one of the founders of the education system in Ontario, was involved in working toward crime prevention with juvenile delinquents.[1] One of the principal drafters of the Juvenile Delinquents Act (J.D.A.), J.J. Kelso, recognized the importance of education:

> Gradually we are coming to see that youthful offenders against criminal law cannot be reclaimed by force but must be won over to a better life by kindness, sympathy and friendly helpfulness; that we should substitute education for punishment and secure the hearty co-operation of the boy or girl in question in his or her own reclamation.[2]

The problem with using education as a tool for rehabilitation in the past was that there were no developed resources for dealing with difficult children, and special education was not a priority.

Over the past two decades, however, there has been a general shift in the philosophy of education professionals to provide better services to children who are "specially challenged."[3] The current debate raging over special education and integration[4] is illustrative of the time and resources being spent on servicing difficult children. As these resources become more developed, the school system becomes more attractive to judges as a means of dealing with young offenders.

The Y.O.A. has not abandoned rehabilitation as a goal in the disposition of offenders, it simply does not give rehabilitation the same paramountcy it enjoyed under the J.D.A.[5] Indeed, section 3(c) of the Y.O.A. recognizes that children have "special needs, and require guidance and assistance." Section 13 allows the court to order the examination of the young person by a "qualified person" to determine whether the young person is suffering from, among other things, "a learning disability or mental retardation." Given the disaffection with rehabilitation through institutionalized care,[6] it is only logical that the courts would turn to the school system to offer a positive alternative.

There are a number of ways in which the rehabilitative aspects of the Y.O.A. affect the school system. The discussion that follows will focus on a few of these aspects — namely, alternative measures, conditions in probation orders, and custodial dispositions.

Alternative Measures

Under the J.D.A., programs were developed on an ad hoc basis to divert juveniles from the court system. This usually involved pre-screening by police officers, and the involvement of a social worker or simply parental discipline. These programs were criticized because of their imprecision and lack of procedural safeguards.[7] The new alternative measures programs under section 4 of the Y.O.A. address these concerns by codifying a procedure for diversion, while encouraging flexibility in the types of programs offered.[8]

Alternative measures, in order to be implemented, must be approved by the attorney general (section 4(1)(a)), and must meet the needs of the young person and the interests of society (section 4(1)(b)). The young person must fully and freely consent to the measures, and be informed of his or her right to instruct counsel before this consent is given (sections 4(1)(c) and (d)). Under section 11(1) it may be necessary to allow the accused to retain and instruct counsel prior to a decision to implement alternative measures, and to have counsel present during any such consideration; the courts are not yet clear on this point. There must also be sufficient evidence to support a criminal charge (section 4(1)(f)), and the young person must acknowledge responsibility for the offence.

These measures are particularly useful when the desire is to impress upon a young person the seriousness of breaking the law, without the trauma of formal judicial proceedings. Take, for example, the situation where a teacher finds out a young person has stolen a watch from the locker room. The student is taken to the principal's office, and the watch is turned over. The police are called and the student is informed of his rights under section 56 of the Y.O.A. The principal could discuss with the police the option of dealing with the child through alternative measures at the school (particularly if it is a first offence), such as writing an essay on the criminal consequences of theft in adult court. The student will have to acknowledge responsibility for the act and face the consequences, without acquiring a criminal record.

Alternative measures are important to the school system because they can be used to ease the burden of involving the police. Following the investigative model discussed in the previous chapter, school officials may find themselves involving the police more often when they discover children breaking the law. This does not mean that every child will then feel the full force of the law. There is the opportunity to avoid the court system through alternative measures. These measures can include many aspects of the school environment such as writing an essay, helping out after school, or attending special counselling sessions.

Probation

Probation orders made under section 20(1)(j) of the Y.O.A. are subject to conditions set out in section 23 of the Act. Section 23(2)(d) provides that young people may be required to "attend school or such other place of learning, training or recreation that would be appropriate" as a condition of probation. Section 23(2)(g) provides flexibility in probation orders by allowing the court to set "such other reasonable conditions ... as the court considers desirable in the circumstances." These conditions can include attendance at school.

Assessment Orders

The widespread use of probation orders offers teachers a unique opportunity to reach children who are difficult to motivate. This use can also be a major challenge and additional burden for teachers. In many cases, young people "act out" because they are experiencing difficulties in school; this acting out can often lead to breaking the law.[9] Section 13 of the Y.O.A. allows for the identification of children with learning disabilities prior to disposition so that any special condition of the offender may be taken into account. Educators can, therefore, use the assessment provisions in section 13 to justify a condition in the probation order that requires the young person to attend remedial or special education classes. In this way, the courts are used to motivate adolescents to learn, because there is the potential of a criminal charge if they breach the probation conditions.

Enforcing School Rules Through Probation

Probation orders may also be used to reinforce school rules. A favourite condition under section 23(2)(g) is that the young person "obey the rules of the school." This provision may become problematic when school rules are not written down, because the order may then be too vague to be enforced. In *R. v. P.D.F.*,[10] Judge Naismith made it clear that conditions in probation orders must be spelled out if the young offender is to be charged with breach of probation under section 26 of the Act. This means that the school rules would have to be clear (that is, written down) and specific instances of breaches should be documented.[11]

Generally, the youth court worker is responsible for supervising a probation order (pursuant to section 37); however, where the school is involved as a condition of probation, it is advisable to stay in contact with the worker and jointly supervise the student. The decision whether to charge an offender with breach of probation will depend largely on the situation of the particular young person involved. However, in general, there is a fair amount of latitude given before charges are laid.

If school authorities feel that a probation order is not working but do not want to lay charges, they may approach the youth court worker to make an application to review the probation order pursuant to section 32(1). A review of an order may be held if there is a material change in circumstances, if the young person is experiencing serious difficulty complying with the terms of the order, if the order will adversely affect the opportunities available to the young person to obtain services, education, or employment, or on any other grounds the court considers appropriate (sections 3(2)(a) to (d)). There is considerable room for discretion.

Identification of a Young Offender

One common complaint we have received from school administrators across the country is that the non-publication of the names of young offenders under section 38 of the Y.O.A. makes it difficult for administrators to find out whether there are, in fact, any young offenders in their schools. To some extent, this problem has been caused by the decision of Justice Reid in *Re Peel Board of Education*[12] in which the court held that holding a suspension or expulsion hearing amounted to publication of the name of the offender and therefore the hearing could not be conducted. As we discussed earlier, that case was more about the presumption of innocence than about publication. In any event, in our opinion the wording of section 38 should not be stretched to exclude youth court workers from communicating fully with school administrators regarding the young offenders in their schools. If the courts are going to use schools as an alternative rehabilitation facility, school administrators must be brought into the rehabilitation team. The school, by necessity, will have to know when a youth is sentenced to three or four months in a custodial institution. This apparently does not violate the spirit or language of section 38. Similarly, school administrators should be fully apprised of any and all probation orders affecting students in their schools. We recommend that administrators actively seek out their local youth court workers to build this "team" relationship.

Custodial Dispositions

The new custodial provisions under section 20(1)(k) pose a particular problem for educators because custody is now used primarily as a means of punishment and deterrence rather than as treatment. The result of this new attitude is that custodial sentences are now designed to "fit the crime" rather than fit the needs of the offender. This is reinforced by section 3(f), which provides for the least possible interference with the freedom of young people. There is a general attitude that imprisonment does little to help put young people on the right track.[13] Judges, therefore, do not always take account of the school year when handing out a custodial disposition and, in general, they will order as short a period of detention as possible in the circumstances. It may be that an offender sentenced in November receives three months in open custody, and finds himself or herself back in school at the beginning of February. The school is then left to devise a suitable program for that young person.

There is no real solution to this problem other than being aware of the difficulties involved and trying to plan ahead. If a young person is to be placed in custody, the court must first consider a pre-disposition report prepared by a youth court worker. Under section 14(2)(c)(vii), this report should include information about the "school attendance and performance record" of the offender. Therefore, in cases where it is undesirable to interrupt a child's school year, this could be made clear to the judge by a letter attached to the pre-disposition report. Judges will, in general, give a considerable amount of weight to a favourable report from a young offender's school.

It should be noted that under the Y.O.A. judges have retained the power to detain young people for the purposes of treatment rather than punishment. It is, however, difficult to implement that power because section 22 requires the consent of the young person. Because these sentences tend to be of greater duration than "punitive" sentences, this consent is often difficult to obtain.[14] The result is to reinforce the punitive aspects of custodial dispositions.

Interference with Dispositions

Section 50 of the Y.O.A. establishes an indictable offence punishable by imprisonment of up to two years for interfering with the disposition of a youth court. No reported cases have yet been decided using this section. It is, however, important for school officials to be aware of these prohibitions in order to avoid an accidental breach. The section prohibits anyone from "inducing or assisting" a young person to leave unlawfully a place of custody, or "knowingly harbouring or concealing" a young person. Therefore, if a young person ran away from a group home and showed up at a teacher's house at 3:00 a.m. looking for a place to stay, it would be a contravention of this section to allow him or her to stay overnight without obtaining the consent of the group home.[15]

Section 50 further prohibits anyone from "inducing or assisting"[16] a young person to breach a condition of a disposition, or "wilfully preventing or interfering with" the performance of a condition contained in a disposition order. If a young offender was required to attend ten special counselling sessions as part of a probation order, and a guidance counsellor felt, after speaking with the young person, that four sessions were sufficient, they are potentially liable to criminal sanction if they did not have the order varied pursuant to section 32. Admittedly, the likelihood of an educator actually being charged is slim, but it is important to be aware of the law in any event.

Teacher as Social Worker

In many areas of the school environment, teachers are expected to act as social workers for the children under their care. This expectation is most prevalent with high school guidance counsellors — teachers who by their very job description fit the social worker role. This role, however, is certainly not limited to guidance counsellors. Teachers often perform the guidance role on an informal basis.

It is the goal of many good teachers to gain the trust and confidence of their students and to help their students develop as individuals in all aspects of their character, not simply academics. Some teachers are more skilled at this than others but most teachers are involved to a certain extent in these child-care functions. Perhaps the first warning for teachers who get involved in this caring aspect of their employment is to be careful not to take on the problems of every child. It is essential that you "care about" the children that you teach, but you cannot be expected to "care for" these children.

Examples of the difficulty in drawing this line can be seen in any school environment. Often at in-services and lectures, we are asked by teachers about their liability for taking actions that involve the trust and confidence of a particular student. For example, what if a student comes to you and is in possession of marijuana, is frightened, and doesn't know what should be done with the drugs. He or she may have unwittingly fallen into possession of these drugs and now the student is caught in a dilemma. He or she has come to you in confidence and expects your help as a "care giver." Many teachers who try to cultivate the trust relationship with their students will be tempted to use their judgment and say to the student, "Go throw this drug away and do not ever get involved with it again." Trusting the relationship with the student, the teacher thinks he or she is in a safe position. This is, however, dangerously close to aiding and abetting a criminal offence. The proper course of action is to bring the student to the principal's office and work out the situation from there with the principal's assistance. It may well be that in many situations, parents should be informed and brought in at some point. Needless to say, these actions may destroy the teacher's trust relationship with the student.

Children will often come to a teacher that they trust and say, "I need to talk to you about something but you have to promise not to tell anybody." Many teachers will foolishly agree to this condition and then they have put themselves in the awkward position of breaching a trust or confidence. If, for example, the child tells you about abuse in the home, you are under a statutory duty to inform the relevant authorities of any information you receive from the child. In short, this promise of confidence should never be given to children. The proper course is to say to the student that you are more than willing to discuss any problem he or she has, that you are willing and open to hear what he or she has to say, but that you cannot guarantee that you will not disclose the information to anyone. Nine times out of ten, the student will proceed to discuss the issue with you, whether or not you give your promise of confidence.

Indiscretion in handling a student's situation (such as those outlined above) may sometimes not result in any criminal sanction but more often in an employment-related sanction. For example, in the case of *Singh v. Board of Reference and Board of School Trustees of School District No. 29, (Lillooet)*,[17] a secondary school teacher was a chaperone at a dance where two female students were taken from the school to a motel by two workmen. The teacher followed and returned the girls to the school. A promise was extracted from the girls that this would not happen again and the teacher promised not to tell their parents. The teacher informed the vice-principal of the events.

The next day the principal, learning of the incident, gave the girls the option of telling their parents within a certain period of time or he would proceed to tell them himself. When the teacher found out about the principal's actions there was a confrontation in the waiting area of the school office in which the teacher shouted "leave her alone — go away — you have done enough damage." The board of reference found that this conduct, in addition to several years of various other incidents of misconduct, constituted just cause for dismissal. The lesson to be learned here is that teachers must always be aware of the potential employment hazards when dealing with students in a confidential setting. The question is: where do a teacher's loyalties lie when offering guidance to a student? Do they lie to the school board as employer, the parent of this child, or the student? The legal and ethical answers may vary depending on the circumstances.

The problem of confidentiality and identifying the client is particularly acute for school guidance counsellors and school psychologists. By their codes of ethics, they may feel that their main duty is to the student as the client who places trust in them. However, in legal terms, both the school board as the employer and the parent may be legally entitled to certain kinds of information about the child, by implication of statute if not by express legal terms. If a student informs the guidance counsellor that she is pregnant and plans to have an abortion, there may be legal problems if the parents or guardians are not informed. The same could be said with respect to a student who is contemplating suicide.

Another problem arises when a student admits to committing a crime or to his or her intention to commit a crime. The admission may raise a duty to the larger school population to inform the principal or other relevant authority so that any risks to other students or the general public can be reduced. Failure to warn in a situation where a student announces a criminal or violent intent could be held to be an act of negligence within the principles discussed in Chapter One. The ethical and legal lines to be drawn by guidance counsellors and teachers at large are complex and little explored.

Reporting Child Abuse

One of the most obvious ways in which a teacher acts as a social worker can be seen in the reporting of child abuse. It is safe to say that most teachers are aware of their statutory obligations to report child abuse; however, not all teachers are aware of the procedures to be followed. Many school boards have established specific protocols for the reporting of abuse and we certainly advise that all boards have these types of policies in place. It may also be helpful, particularly for elementary-level teachers, to insist on an in-service with local police authorities and social workers to establish clearly the lines of communications that should be followed when reporting an abuse situation. Most board protocols require teachers to bring the matter to the attention of the school principal and let the school principal handle the reporting. Even if this is the protocol in a particular

school, a teacher should still be aware of the actual process. Most of
the reporting laws in Canada, in fact, identify the individuals or
authorities to whom the report must be made and in the opinion of
some academics this report must be made by the teacher, regardless
of internal school procedures. Certainly provincial legislation is
paramount over any particular school board policy. It is perhaps
advisable in cases where a teacher feels it necessary to report a
situation of abuse to report his or her suspicion to the principal first,
and then in conjunction with the principal, contact the appropriate
authorities.

The first issue to be addressed with regard to reporting abuse is
the issue of what must be reported. The laws in each province differ
in this respect and, to make it more complicated, none of the laws in
Canada provides any convenient explanation of what constitutes
"child abuse" for the purposes of reporting.[18] Teachers are naturally
reticent to involve the outside authorities and create the kind of
trauma that is brought on by a child abuse investigation and this
reticence is made worse by the lack of a discernible standard for child
abuse. There is also concern about the reaction of parents who are
the object of suspicion.

In order to establish a definition, one must define the meaning of
"child" under the legislation. In Manitoba, a "child" is a person under
the age of majority; in New Brunswick and Prince Edward Island, it
is a person actually or apparently under the age of majority; it is a
person under the age of 19 in British Columbia; and a person under
the age of 18 in Alberta, Ontario, and Quebec. In the Northwest
Territories and Nova Scotia, a "child" is a person under the age of 16.
In Saskatchewan and Newfoundland, it is defined as a person who
is actually or apparently under the age of 16.

The definition of "abuse" is slightly more abstract and most of the
statutes use broad and vague terminology to identify the range of
specific behaviours and conditions that may create child abuse.
There is general agreement that conduct qualifying as child abuse
can be divided into four major categories. Professor Foster provides
the following guidance in a useful article.[19]

> (i) physical abuse — which includes "any physical force or action
> which results in or may potentially result in a non-accidental injury to
> a child and which exceeds that which could be considered reasonable
> discipline";[20]
>
> (ii) emotional maltreatment — which includes the acting out by
> those responsible for the welfare of a child or their negative or ambigu-
> ous feelings towards the child (through, for example, constantly
> chastising, blaming, belittling, ridiculing, humiliating or rejecting a

child, or persistently displaying a lack of concern for the child's welfare) which results in some degree of emotional damage to the child;[21]

(iii) sexual abuse — which includes "any sexual touching, sexual intercourse or sexual exploitation of a child and may include any sexual behaviour directed toward a child";[22] and

(iv) neglect, physical or emotional — which includes "failure on the part of those responsible for the care of the child to provide for the physical, emotional or medical needs of a child to the extent that the child's health, development or safety is endangered."[23]

In addition to these aspects of child abuse, some of these statutes make specific reference to the actual perpetrator of the abuse as being relevant to a determination of the reporting requirement. In the Northwest Territories and Quebec, the relationship of the abuser to the victim is applicable in only some forms of reportable abuse. In Alberta, Ontario, Prince Edward Island, Manitoba, and Saskatchewan, the relationship of the abuser to the victim is an essential ingredient. Generally, the abuser must be a parent, guardian, or person who has the care or charge of the child. Again, we recommend that teachers check the statutory provisions within their province as well as the school board regulations to determine the particular requirements that apply to the nature of the abuse and the identity of the abuser in their jurisdiction.

Another issue that arises in the reporting of abuse is the extent of knowledge required to trigger the reporting obligation. In British Columbia, Northwest Territories, Ontario, Prince Edward Island, and Quebec, the teacher's duty to report arises when he or she has "reasonable grounds to believe" or "reasonable grounds to suspect" abuse. The statutes all contain different wording but the common denominator is the use of the phrase "reasonable." This creates an objective standard or test for whether the reporting should be made in any given situation.

In contrast, the provincial laws in New Brunswick and Alberta provide that the reporting requirement is triggered only when the educator personally believes or suspects that a child is the victim of abuse. This is a subjective standard in which there is no test for whether the suspicion is "reasonable" or not; it is simply the judgment call of the particular teacher. In Manitoba, Newfoundland, Nova Scotia, and Saskatchewan, there is a stricter requirement: all information suggesting that a child may be the subject of abuse must be reported. This means that there is no requirement that the teacher reasonably believe or suspect that the child is, in fact, being abused but simply that the teacher must report any information that indicates a need for protection of a child. Again, teachers are encouraged to involve their principals or other school administrators when they determine whether to report the alleged abuse. It should also be noted that once the duty arises, the reporting should be done as quickly as possible. Most of the statutes make reference to "forthwith" or "without delay," which indicate an immediate reporting of all relevant information.

In most statutory structures the person reporting the abuse is protected from legal action from the person who is the object of the report. This is true even if the suspicions of abuse prove unfounded at the end of the day. Under the Nova Scotia statute, as one example, a person making a child abuse report attracts legal liability only if the report was made in bad faith.[24]

Truancy

Another aspect of the social working role of teachers is the efforts made by school personnel to combat truancy. Although, traditionally, truancy may have been seen as simply a matter of rounding up "delinquent" children, in the modern education environment it is recognized as a much more complex issue.[25] There are a number of varying models of truancy that attribute the cause to a wide variety of factors including the home environment of the student, the socio-economic position of the student, unsociability and unhappiness, as well as recognizing the school environment itself as a cause for absenteeism.[26]

We do not propose in this book to delve into the complexities of truancy and the argument over its cause and effect. It is safe to say that truancy is a prevalent problem and that students certainly cannot succeed at school if they are not going to school. Teachers, although not the primary agents for enforcing school attendance, can serve a useful purpose in their social welfare role to help identify the causes of truancy in particular students and perhaps avoid truant behaviour before it starts. It is usually the classroom teacher that has the front-line contact and close experience with students, particularly at the elementary level. These teachers are in a good position to assess the signs of truant behaviour. The classroom teacher may also have more access to the parents and, therefore, may perhaps have more effect than a principal or truancy officer.

In addition to these general considerations, the legislative trends over the last 10 years are to put truancy in the family court arena, much the same as children's services legislation. In Alberta, the courts have refused to interpret the section that requires every child between 6 and 16 to attend school as creating a legal duty punishable on summary conviction where that duty is not carried out.[27] The court reviewed other provincial legislation and concluded that only Ontario and New Brunswick created an offence for a truant child and, even then, not in clear language. The court was persuaded by the legislative movement toward empowering family court to make orders for attendance rather than to punish on summary conviction. Alternatively, many provinces make it an offence for parents to allow their child not to attend school. These provisions have been challenged under the Charter as potentially violating the parents' freedom of religion,[28] although the courts have ultimately upheld the requirement that children attend some form of provincially approved schooling.

Teacher as Child Advocate[29]

We have looked at the teacher as a rehabilitation counsellor and as a social worker and now we examine the teacher's social welfare role as an informal lawyer or advocate for the child. Every individual in the caring professions who comes in contact with children feels a natural tendency, particularly toward vulnerable children, to take on some form of advocacy role. It may be that the teacher simply is acting as an advocate within the school system to achieve better service for the child or the teacher may well extend that role into seeking out external resources such as Children's Aid, United Way, or Big Brothers/Big Sisters, to name but a few. In much the same way that the education system has expanded and diversified, so too have the external government agencies that affect children. In earlier, simpler days, child advocacy was a rather simple task given that the only resources that could be drawn upon were those of the community in which the child lived. In today's more complex world of varying institutions to help children, the child advocacy role becomes much more complex.

Given the day-to-day contact of classroom teachers with their pupils, they are natural advocates for children with special needs. Often children of single-parent or lower-income families need the help of an articulate advocate to obtain necessary services. Anyone who has dealt with the bureaucratic tangles that can be created by some of the child welfare agencies will be well aware of this need. As in any bureaucratic structure, as the system gets larger, the individuals within the system may focus too much on the delivery of service on a "macro" level as opposed to the "micro" needs of particular children. This is particularly true in the age of government cutbacks — when every social welfare agency is struggling to justify its existence to achieve government-funding success.

It is important to realize that advocacy is not necessarily adversarial. It is not always necessary for teachers to feel that they must "take on the system," whether it is the educational system or the larger external social welfare system. Often the most effective form of advocacy is the simple co-opting and coordinating of resisting forces. From an employment standpoint, it is also wiser to take the more subtle approach than to risk unnecessary annoyance of individuals in the government hierarchy. This is especially true of internal advocacy within the school system. It may also be helpful in this regard for teachers as a group to encourage their school system to view child advocacy as a positive employment objective and one that fits with the role of the teacher rather than labelling teacher advocates as "disturbers."

One good example of teachers acting as advocates for children in the school system is provided by a recent program in the Peel Board of Education where the teachers in an elementary school created a "breakfast club" for their students. It was noted on regular occasions by classroom teachers that particular children were having difficulty concentrating in class and were consistently being disciplined for acting out. Finally, when the principal asked one of the children whether he had been given breakfast that morning, the child stated that he normally was not able to have breakfast in the morning.

Over a number of weeks, the school implemented a program where each classroom teacher was instructed to keep a close eye on children who they felt may be at risk of not being properly fed in the morning. Without singling the children out, they were discreetly sent to the main office (often with the excuse of bringing the attendance record to the office) and, once there, they were asked whether they had breakfast and, if not, they were fed. The discipline problems in this particular school declined substantially as a result of this breakfast club, and this program is now being adopted in other schools. This is an excellent example of classroom teachers' and administrators' identifying a specific child welfare need that requires a solution. Clearly, the parents were not in a position to help and it was not the kind of problem that could be necessarily solved through any of the institutional social welfare agencies. Although the schools certainly cannot replace these agencies, this model of identifying problems and advocating solutions is an important and positive role for teachers in the school system.

In many instances, the advocacy role will involve the coordination of existing agencies rather than the creation of new programs within the school. Often, parents simply need to be directed to the appropriate agency and assisted in some way with advocating within that agency in order to improve the welfare of the child. For instance, children whose parents are illiterate are certainly disadvantaged by not having proper role models at home to encourage and assist them in their studies. In this situation, a teacher can often be helpful by directing a parent to a community literacy program that would benefit both the parent and the child. Such suggestions must, of course, be made with sensitivity. It is the constant contact between teacher and student that provides the opportunity for teachers to assess the needs of families in these situations.

One particular problem with respect to teenage students that should be emphasized is the danger of a teacher's acting as an advocate in young offender situations. Section 56(6) of the Y.O.A. states that an adult consulted pursuant to section 56(2)(c) shall be deemed not to be a person in authority for the purposes of the admissibility of a statement under section 56. As we discussed in the last chapter, section 56(2)(c) allows a young person to consult a parent or, in the absence of a parent, any other appropriate adult chosen by the young person before giving a statement. Often, the individual of choice for a student will be a teacher whom the student trusts within the school. The teacher, taking on his or her natural advocacy role, may be tempted to act in this advisory capacity when requested by the student, particularly when the police are at the scene and the student is visibly shaken. However, the danger in assuming this role is that, according to this paragraph, the teacher is not required to give any warning to the child and any statement made by the child will be admissible as evidence in court.

Therefore, if the teacher consults with the student before formal questioning and the student confesses, the Crown prosecutor may subpoena the teacher consulted and the teacher will be required on the witness stand to relate the statement given by the student. Teachers as advocates unfortunately are not protected by the solicitor-client privilege that is enjoyed by lawyers. Therefore, if a teacher truly wishes to assist an accused young person in the absence of his or her parent, we recommend that the student be directed to a local legal aid service for advice.

Teacher as Family Mediator

Given the epidemic of broken families in today's society, teachers are often faced with difficult family law-related issues when dealing with the children in their classrooms. Often the teacher may be caught in the middle of trying to assist a child in dealing with a broken home as well as having to deal with both parents simultaneously. Generally, provided that neither parent has been absolutely denied access, they both have general rights with regard to input into the education of their child, as well as access to student records. Perhaps more troublesome than input into a child's education is the actual day-to-day custodial problems that arise when different parents are arriving at the school to pick up their child. The Criminal Code contains provisions that penalize the taking of the child by someone other than the person or persons with lawful custody, whether or not there is a court order with respect to custody:

> 280. (1) Every one who, without lawful authority, takes or causes to be taken an unmarried person under the age of sixteen years out of the possession of and against the will of the parent or guardian of that person or of that person or of any other person who has the lawful care or charge of that person is guilty of an indictable offence and liable to imprisonment for a term not exceeding five years.
>
> (2) In this section and sections 281 to 283, "guardian" includes any person who has in law or in fact the custody or control of another person. ...
>
> 282. Every one who, being the parent, guardian or person having the lawful care or charge of a person under the age of fourteen years, takes, entices away, conceals, detains, receives or harbours that person, in contravention of the custody provisions of a custody order in relation to that person made by a court anywhere in Canada, with intent to deprive a parent or guardian, or any other person who has the lawful care or charge of that person, of the possession of that person is guilty of
>
>> (a) an indictable offence and liable to imprisonment for a term not exceeding ten years; or
>>
>> (b) an offence punishable on summary conviction.

Defences to the crime of abduction are specifically set out in sections 284 and 285 of the Criminal Code, which provide that no one shall be found guilty of the offence of abduction if they can satisfy the court that the taking of the young person was done with consent or if they can establish that the taking was necessary to protect the young person from danger or imminent harm. Section 286 states that the consent of the young person to the conduct of the accused does not afford a defence. The defence of parental consent contained in section 284 raises interpretation problems. Who can consent to the taking of a child? Is it the parent who has temporary lawful custody, such as a father exercising his rights of access, or the parent who has permanent custody, such as a mother who may disagree with her former husband? These complicated questions emphasize the difficulty in predicting a court's interpretation of the law and the importance of preventive action.

If the non-custodial parent wishes to pick up a child from the school, the teacher or principal should get in touch with the parent who does have custody before allowing the child to leave. If the custodial parent objects to the child's accompanying the other parent, it is probably advisable to ask him or her to come to the school and bring any applicable court orders concerning custody. If a dispute seems likely, it may also be wise to notify the police, whose function it is to ensure that court orders are obeyed. Ideally, the teacher or principal should obtain legal advice when both parents claim the right to take the child, although such advice is not always quickly available. Although teachers may be required to act as mediators in parental disputes over a child regarding education, educators should never attempt to adjudicate parental disputes over rights of custody or access.

Once a parent has been awarded exclusive custody of a child, he or she has the right to make decisions that relate to the child's upbringing — including how and where the child will be educated.[30] However, under the Divorce Act, the access parent also has some rights with respect to the child's education.[31] A custody order usually grants the parent the right to give a consent (medical or otherwise) on behalf of the child. The parent without custody is not permitted to interfere in the child's upbringing even though he or she may have access to the child and the right to some involvement. If there is any question about which parent is able to give permission for the child to partake in an activity or enrol in a course, the teacher should ask to see a copy of the relevant custody order if it exists. In many cases, it may be the wisest course of action simply to put the problem in the hands of the principal.

It should be noted that the non-custodial parent may still exercise many rights as a legal guardian of the child and these rights should be carefully balanced wherever possible. Although it will differ from situation to situation given the particular circumstances of a child, it is in many cases in the best interest of the child for the teacher to make efforts to involve both parents to whatever extent possible in the education of their children. Amendments to the federal Divorce Act in 1986 make it possible for the courts to award "joint custody" to parents and this requires even more sensitivity on the part of teachers because both parents will want to exercise equal rights with regard to the education of their children.

Teacher as Para-Medic

Although a teacher is normally not trained to provide medical services, they are often called upon to do so. In Chapter One, we discussed the role of the teacher in providing first aid when a student has been injured in an accident. In the discussion of integrating disabled students in Chapter Two, one of the related services identified to make schools truly accessible was the provision of medication. This service has in the past been focused on the special education classroom but, with the advent of mainstreaming, it has become a matter of more general concern.

In legal terms, it is dangerous for a teacher to be providing medical services that fall outside the range of his or her professional competence. Although such services should be provided by a school employee — for example, a nurse — the teacher should not engage in medical practice.[32] In terms of negligence, the teacher is assuming a large risk when providing medical services. It is for this reason that most teacher associations advise against playing a medical role.

One of the most frequent ways that this problem arises is with respect to the dispensing of medications in the classroom. This should be done very carefully and it is wise to have the parents provide the doctor's instructions with respect to any prescribed medication. As part of a teacher's role, they should be prepared to deal with students who are epileptic, diabetic, or subject to other physical disabilities. They should be trained to deal with an emergency situation both for the benefit of the child and to guard against legal actions.

As schools include more students with physical and mental disabilities, the range of medical problems to which teachers are exposed is growing. The integration of these disabled children also means that a wide range of classroom teachers are confronted with students with a variety of medical needs. Schools need to develop clearer rules and policies in this important area and provide the necessary medical supports for the teacher. The lack of clear guidance at the present time with respect to the teacher's para-medical role causes anxiety in the teacher and raises the spectre of liability for negligent conduct.

Summary

In summary, there are many varied roles exercised by teachers as social welfare agents. Often these roles arise simply as a result of a teacher's constant and intimate contact with their students. As caring professionals, teachers should at least be aware of the opportunities to take action on behalf of children in these different capacities aside from the narrower duty of providing an education. They should also become more aware of the legal implications in adopting such social welfare roles with respect to their students. This is one of the new frontiers in education law.

ENDNOTES

1. Jeffrey Leon, "The Development of Canadian Juvenile Justice: A Background for Reform," in *Osgoode Hall Law Journal* (1977), vol. 15, no. 1, 71, at 81.

2. J.J. Kelso, "Delinquent Children: Some Improved Methods Whereby They May Be Prevented from Following a Criminal Career," in *Canadian Law Review* (1907), vol. 6, no. 3, at 106.

3. Terri Sussel and Michael Manley-Casimir, "Special Education and the Charter: The Right to Equal Benefit of the Law," in *Canadian Journal of Law and Society* (1987), vol. 2, at 45.

4. A. Wayne MacKay and Gordon Krinke, "Education as a Basic Human Right: A Response to Special Education and the Charter," in *Canadian Journal of Law and Society* (1987), vol. 2, at 73.

5. Peter Gabor, Ian Greene, and Peter McCormick, "The Young Offenders Act: The Alberta Youth Court Experience in the First Year," in *Canadian Journal of Family Law* (1986), vol. 5, 301, at 306.

6. George Thomson, "The Child in Conflict with Society" (1973), 11 R.F.L. 257, at 258.

7. Mark Berlin and Herbert Allard, "Diversion of Children from the Juvenile Courts," in *Canadian Journal of Family Law* (1980), vol. 3, at 439.

8. Bala and Lilles, *The Young Offenders Act Annotated* (Toronto: Butterworths, 1986), at 38.

9. Federal Ministry of the Solicitor General, "Young Offenders Act" (excerpt from a paper prepared for the CACLD), in *Just Cause*, vol. 3, no. 2 (Winter 1985), 15, at 16.

10. *R. v. P.D.F.* (1987), 57 C.R. (3d) 22 (Ont. Prov. Ct.).

11. It is advisable that school rules be written down in any event; see A. Wayne MacKay and Lyle I. Sutherland, "Making and Enforcing School Rules in the Wake of the Charter of Rights," in Y.L. Jack Lam, ed., *Canadian Public Education System: Issues and Prospects* (Calgary: Detselig Enterprises Limited, 1990).

12. *Re Peel Board of Education et al.* (1987), 59 O.R. (2d) 654 (H.C.J.).

13. Jim Hackler, "The Impact of the Y.O.A.," in *Canadian Journal of Criminology* (1987), vol. 29, no. 2, 205, at 208.

14. The consent requirement in the Y.O.A. has been severely criticized, even by adolescents themselves: see P.G. Jaffe, A. Leschied, and J.L. Farthing, "Youth's Knowledge and Attitudes about the

Y.O.A.: Does Anyone Care What They Think?" in *Canadian Journal of Criminology* (1987), vol. 29, no. 3, 309, at 314.

15. To be guilty of an offence, the teacher would have to know that the young person had escaped lawful custody: see *R. v. Chernish* (1954), 109 C.C.C. 398 (Ont. C.A.).

16. The Supreme Court of Canada has defined "assisting" as meaning the encouragement of the offence; an act that facilitates its commission, or hinders its prevention: see *Dunlop and Sylvester v. The Queen* (1979), 47 C.C.C. (2d) 93 (S.C.C.).

17. (1987), *School Law Commentary*, Case File No. 3-5-8 (B.C.S.C.).

18. Examples of the relevant statutory provisions include the following: Family and Child Services Act, S.P.E.I. 1981, c. F-2.01 (as amended by S.P.E.I. 1988, c. 20, s. 14); Child and Family Services Act, S.S. 1989-90, c. C-7.2, s. 12; Child Welfare Act, S.N. 1972, c. 37, s. 49; Family and Children Services Act, R.S.O. 1990, c. C.11, s. 72; Child and Family Services Act, S.M. 1989-90, c. 3, s. 18; Child and Family Services Act, S.B.C. 1980, c. 11, s. 7; Child Welfare Act, S.A. 1984, c. 8.1, s. 3; Family Services Act, S.N.B. 1988, c. F-2.2, s. 30; and Children and Family Services Act, S.N.S. 1990, c. 5, s. 25.

19. W.F. Foster, "Child Abuse in Schools: Legal Obligations of School Teachers, Administrators and Boards," paper presented to the National CAPSLE Conference in Vancouver, British Columbia, April 29 to May 2, 1990, at 2.

20. T.L. MacGuire and D.S. McCall, *Child Abuse: A Manual for Schools* (Vancouver: EduServ, 1987), at III-2.

21. Ibid., at III-5.

22. Ibid., at III-2.

23. Ibid.

24. Children and Family Services Act, S.N.S. 1990, c. 5, s. 25.

25. David Brown, "Truants, Families and Schools: A Critique on the Literature on Truancy," in *Educational Review* (1983), vol. 35, no. 3.

26. Audrey Dean, "The Attendance Board: An Alternative to Taking Truancy to Court," a paper presented to the National CAPSLE Conference, supra endnote 18.

27. *In the matter of K.G.* (1987), *School Law Commentary*, Case File No. 2-1-6 (Alta. Prov. Ct.).

28. *R. v. Jones*, [1986] 2 S.C.R. 284.

29. The teacher's role as advocate is very well described by Margo Herbert, "Who Speaks for the Children," paper presented to the 1991 C.A.P.S.L.E. Conference in Edmonton, Alberta.

30. Robinson, "Custody and Access," in E. Mendes da Costa, ed., *Studies in Canadian Family Law* (Toronto: Butterworths, 1972), at 546.

31. Divorce Act, R.S.C. 1985, c. 3 (2d Supp.), s. 16(5).

32. W. MacKay, "The Charter of Rights and Special Education: Blessing or Curse," in *Canadian Journal of Exceptional Children* (1977), vol. 3, at 118-27.

5

Teachers as Employees

This final chapter deals with the teacher's rights and responsibilities in the context of labour law. The preceding chapters have focused primarily on duties and responsibilities of teachers with regard to other people in the education system. This chapter focuses more on the teacher's own rights in the school system. We will discuss the rights of freedom of expression, privacy and lifestyle, and freedom of association as they relate to teachers in the school setting. We will also discuss and review the rights and responsibilities of teachers in the employment and labour law aspects of their work. In general, teachers are subject to a wide range of responsibilities from a number of distinct sources. This is compounded by the fact that the role and legal status of teachers in Canada has not, to date, been seriously addressed or dealt with by legislation.

Legal Rights of Teachers

The legal rights of teachers in Canada are drawn primarily from the Charter of Rights, the relevant education statutes, the various provincial human rights codes, and labour law (both common law and statutory). It is an interesting twist that, although teachers are subject to scrutiny under the Charter in their handling of students, they may benefit from the rights and freedoms guaranteed by the Charter when dealing with their employers. We will examine the dynamics of this relationship in this chapter.

Our discussion of teachers' rights issues will be primarily within the framework of the Charter of Rights; however, some of the cases used may be drawn from decisions of human rights tribunals. There is some overlap between protection by human rights codes and the Charter of Rights, and teachers generally will have the option to choose the appropriate forum. Although the principles are similar, the dispute resolution system and remedies in human rights legislation are radically different from those under the Charter. Human rights legislation conciliates and mediates problems, and the government of each province pays the costs of having a human rights officer investigate and mediate. Only as a last resort will a tribunal be set up to hear the complaint in an adversarial setting. The remedies available are limited and most often simply involve monetary compensation[1] and directions for appropriate behaviour in future.[2]

The Charter, on the other hand, is the "supreme law of Canada" and, under section 24, the courts have the power to grant any remedy that is "just and appropriate in the circumstances." Furthermore, section 52 of the Constitution Act, 1982 allows the courts to strike down portions of legislation, at any governmental level, that are inconsistent with the Charter. This provides a more substantial legal remedy for the enforcement of rights because the courts are free to strike out portions of the provincial education acts. Such a statutory attack is difficult under the human rights legislation. The Charter also applies nationally, whereas provincial human rights codes apply only within the respective province.[3] Teachers and teacher associations are therefore more likely to use the substantial powers of the Charter than human rights legislation to challenge school board action when they wish to set a useful precedent for the future.

Freedom of Expression

Section 2(b) of the Charter guarantees everyone freedom of thought, belief, opinion, and expression. This section has been given broad interpretation by the Supreme Court of Canada. Freedom of expression has "both content and form" and includes any "activity which conveys or attempts to convey meaning."[4] It therefore includes expression through conduct and dress as well as through actual speech. For teachers, freedom of expression breaks down into two categories: expression within the school and expression outside the school.

School boards will need to rely on the reasonable limits in section 1 of the Charter to curtail teachers' freedom of speech rights. Primarily within the school, section 1 will be used to require teachers to express themselves within the confines of approved curricula. This was an issue raised in Alberta where a teacher chose to teach students in his history class that the Holocaust in World War II was a hoax. He was fired, and his termination was upheld by a justice of the Alberta Queen's Bench.[5] More difficult issues arise where, for example, a teacher places an anti-abortion poster on his or her door, or wears unorthodox clothing. Normally, the Charter can protect these activities. This, however, depends on their disruptive potential. One formulation of the test for freedom of expression in schools discussed earlier is whether it causes a "material or substantial disruption" in the classroom.[6] Perhaps this will be employed to place limits on teachers.

It will be more difficult for school boards to argue reasonable limits on freedom of expression outside the school because this involves a less direct impact on the school environment. However, where the expression outside the school is published and is seriously controversial, teachers can be liable for censorship and dismissal. In a recent decision, the New Brunswick Human Rights Board of Inquiry held that a New Brunswick teacher who had published a number of anti-semitic books as well as letters to the editor that claimed that the Holocaust was a myth, violated the human rights legislation. Malcolm Ross, the teacher in question, taught mathematics in the school and, therefore, did not have occasion to teach his views directly in the classroom. Although he did not advocate these views in school, the Human Rights Board of Inquiry found that his writings had impaired his ability as a teacher and the school board was ordered immediately to put him on leave of absence without pay for a period of 18 months to attempt to find him a non-teaching position. If a non-teaching position was not available or not accepted, his employment was to be terminated.[7] Initially, the board imposed a "gag order" prohibiting Ross from producing anti-semitic materials; however, this was struck down by the New Brunswick Court of Queen's Bench.[8]

A common problem that involves freedom of expression both inside and outside the school is the criticism of employers and fellow teachers. Criticisms of employers can put teachers in a vulnerable position because they may be construed as "insubordination" and make teachers subject to discipline proceedings (that is, suspension). This is particularly true in cases where the criticism occurs within the school setting.[9] It will be more difficult to make out a case for discipline where the comments are made outside of school,[10] unless the comments are so critical and inflammatory that they impair the teacher's ability to teach, or lead to a public perception of inability to teach.[11] Criticisms of fellow teachers are restricted by statute or regulation in most provinces as well as in the various codes of professional conduct:

> s. 18(1) A member shall,
> (a) avoid interfering with in an unwarranted manner between other teachers and pupils;

(b) on making an adverse report on another member, furnish
him/her with a written statement of the report at the earliest
possible time and not later than three days after making the
report ...[12]

A similar provision has recently been upheld by the British Columbia
Court of Appeal.[13] In that case, a teacher showed up at the parents'
association meeting of another school (where her children were in
attendance) and criticized the actions and teaching techniques of a
teacher in the school. The court found that even though the teacher
was speaking as a parent, she was required to respect the Code of
Ethics restrictions on criticism of colleagues. Thus there are professional limits on the freedom of expression of teachers.

Privacy and Lifestyle

The privacy and lifestyles of teachers may cause difficulty with
employers and, consequently, lead to court challenges. The Charter
arguments advanced here will involve the protection of "liberty" and
"security of the person" under section 7,[14] and freedom of expression
under section 2.[15] Teachers are under constant scrutiny in their
communities because parents are extremely sensitive about who is
setting an example for their children. This was brought to light
recently in *Abbotsford School District 34 Board of School Trustees v.
Shewan and Shewan*.[16] In that case a teacher posed half-nude for a
picture taken by her husband, who was also a teacher, and the
picture was published in an American magazine. Both teachers were
suspended for one month without pay. The B.C. Supreme Court
upheld the suspension, stating that the standard of conduct to be
met by teachers was that of the community in which they taught. The
B.C. Court of Appeal dismissed the appeal, stating that teachers hold
a position of trust and responsibility, and their conduct cannot be
permitted to jeopardize public confidence in the school system. A
similar situation in Quebec concerning nude photographs of teachers did not produce any sanction.

Another restriction on the lifestyle of teachers can be seen in cases
where teachers breach the provisions of the Criminal Code. Most
collective agreements allow school boards to dismiss teachers if they
are convicted of a criminal offence. In serious cases such as sexual
assault, the basis is obvious and relatively easy to enforce.[17]
However, it is more difficult to justify dismissal in subtle cases such
as possession of marijuana[18] or impaired driving. The test generally
is whether the subject matter of the offence is inconsistent with one's
continued duties as a teacher.

The legal challenge is to strike a proper balance between the privacy rights of the teacher and the legitimate interests of the employing school board in ensuring that teachers provide a proper role model for students. The expectation of teachers as moral exemplars in the community is not only a public expectation but part of the statutory definition of the duties of a teacher.[19] As part of the nature of teaching, there are limitations on the public conduct of teachers. In Charter terms, the question is: what limitations on the free expression and liberty of teachers can be justified as reasonable in the light of their professional duty to act as role models for their students? Another question is: what private conduct is relevant?[20]

Freedom of Association

Freedom of association is protected by section 2(d) of the Charter. In at least one respect, it can raise issues of lifestyle because teachers may be subject to censure if they were to associate with a group — such as a gay rights group — that was frowned upon by their school board. This can certainly become a problem if the teacher is employed in a particularly conservative community, because the *Shewan* case indicates that the local community standard applies. As yet, there have been few courtroom confrontations in this area, and the possible restrictions on association are open to speculation.[21]

A more concrete problem for teachers in this area is the freedom "not to associate." In every province, teachers' contracts are regulated through collective bargaining legislation and the profession is very much a "closed shop." In Ontario, for example, there are a number of different teachers' federations, but there are no membership options. Every teacher is a member of the Ontario Teachers' Federation, and bylaw I of this federation mandates the affiliate organization for different classes of teachers. There are five affiliate groups: Federation of Women Teachers' Association of Ontario (F.W.T.A.O.), Ontario Secondary School Teachers' Federation (O.S.S.T.F.), Ontario Public School Teachers' Federation (O.P.S.T.F.), Ontario English Catholic Teachers' Federation (O.E.C.T.A.), and the l'Association des enseignants franco-ontariens (A.E.F.O.).

This mandatory division of teachers has been challenged under section 2(d) and section 15 (equality rights) of the Charter in the Ontario courts.[22] A female teacher complained to the court that she was not permitted to join the O.P.S.T.F. because of bylaw I (which required her to join the F.W.T.A.O.) and sought a remedy under the Charter.[23] Justice Ewaschuk held that the Charter did not apply to the situation because bylaw I could not be characterized as government action. Although membership in the parent organization (O.T.F.) was required by the Teaching Profession Act,[24] the bylaw in question was developed through the internal organization of the O.T.F. and was too far removed from government to be protected by the Charter.

Another example where the freedom "not to associate" may become an issue is in situations where the teachers' federation takes on a political stance outside the realm of education. For example, the O.S.S.T.F. has adopted policy statements on nuclear disarmament, pornography, and hazardous wastes. What if they adopt a resolution on abortion? Would a teacher be forced to pay union dues to an organization that used this money to advocate causes that the teacher did not support? The Ontario Court of Appeal recently ruled in a case involving the Ontario Public Service Employees Union that the use of union dues was a private matter and beyond the reach of the Charter.[25] This reasoning could easily be applied to teachers' federations as well.

Equality Rights

Section 15 of the Charter guarantees equality and specifically prohibits discrimination on the basis of a number of enumerated grounds.[26] Some of these enumerated grounds, such as age, sex, and physical disability, are particularly relevant for teachers.

The prohibition against age discrimination has been used to challenge mandatory retirement policies in a number of cases involving university professors with differing results. The Supreme Court of Canada, in a series of rulings discussed earlier,[27] held that mandatory retirement policies violated section 15 of the Charter. These policies, however, were upheld as a reasonable limit pursuant to section 1.

Another important aspect of section 15 is the protection for teachers with physical disabilities. The extent of the protection will be to require school boards to accommodate physical disability where the disability does not amount to a "bona fide work requirement." The test for this requirement has been outlined in general by the Supreme Court of Canada:

> To be a bona fide occupational qualification and requirement a limitation ... must be imposed honestly, in good faith, and in the sincerely held belief that such limitation is imposed in the interests of the adequate performance of the work involved with all reasonable dis-

patch, safety and economy, and not for ulterior or extraneous reasons aimed at objectives which could defeat the purpose of the [human rights] Code. In addition it must be related in an objective sense to the performance of the employment concerned, in that it is reasonably necessary to assure the efficient and economical performance of the job without endangering the employee, his fellow employees and the general public.[28]

This has not been specifically tested in the school setting, but presumably this reasoning will apply to require reasonable access for teachers with physical disabilities.

A more recent and politically sensitive issue in the area of physical disability is the presence of teachers who are HIV-positive or have AIDS (acquired immune deficiency syndrome) in the classroom. The current legal trend, both in Canada and in the United States, is to classify persons with the HIV virus as "disabled" and, therefore, subject to human rights protection.[29] In Nova Scotia, the issue was brought to the fore in a rural community where a young teacher was found to be carrying the HIV virus. He was initially reassigned to non-teaching duties (under the threat of a boycott by parents) but was eventually appointed to a provincial task force on AIDS to diffuse the difficult situation.[30] School boards and provincial governments across the country are faced with the challenge over the next few years of educating the public on this issue and formulating policies that respect the rights of infected individuals.[31]

Discrimination on the basis of sex has been tested in the courts in the past, and is likely to be the object of further discussion. In *Nevio Rossi v. School District No. 57*,[32] a male teacher applied for a job teaching physical education to female students. The school board refused his application because they claimed the job required a female instructor. The Human Rights Council in British Columbia held that the school board could not prove that being female was a necessary requirement for the job and awarded damages to the teacher.[33]

It is now clearly established that discrimination on the basis of pregnancy is also discrimination on the basis of sex. Surprisingly, in an early Supreme Court of Canada decision, the court held that distinctions based on pregnancy did not constitute sex discrimination. This decision was based on the Canadian Bill of Rights but the Supreme Court has reached a different conclusion under the Charter in *Brooks v. Canada Safeway Ltd.*[34] The protection of pregnant women in the workplace has been further extended by both statutes and judicial decisions.[35] These additional protections for pregnant women are as applicable to teachers as to any other employees.

Another aspect of sexual discrimination that will test the limits of section 15 of the Charter is the use of affirmative action in hiring policies. Traditionally in Canada, the upper administrative levels of education have been male dominated. Many school boards may therefore wish to offer superintendent positions and principalships to women on a preferential basis. Section 15(2) allows such policies:

> 15(2). Subsection (1) does not preclude any law, program or activity that has as its object the amelioration of conditions of disadvantaged individuals or groups including those that are disadvantaged because of race, national or ethnic origin, colour, religion, sex, age or mental or physical disability.

As yet there has not been any explicit reliance on this subsection of the Charter by school boards. Affirmative action policies could also be used to hire more teachers from visible minorities and the First Nations without running afoul of the Charter equality guarantees.

Dismissal for Denominational Cause

The unique denominational school structure in the various provincial education systems often gives rise to difficult questions about the denominational rights of teachers. This area of teachers' rights is a prime example of the blend of Charter issues, human rights statutes, and labour law in the field of education. Simply stated, the problem arises when a teacher employed by a Roman Catholic separate school board violates some aspect of the religious faith. Separate school boards have traditionally claimed the legal authority to dismiss these teachers, because they feel that these teachers undermine the underlying purpose of separate schools.

In legal terms, dismissing teachers for denominational cause is a battle between two constitutional standards. The first is contained in section 93 of the original Constitution Act, 1867, which protects the rights of the province to establish a separate school system.[36] This section is fortified by section 29 of the Charter, which states that nothing in the Charter derogates from or abrogates any of the rights in the constitution respecting denominational schools.[37] The other side of the issue is that teachers are entitled to freedom of conscience and religion pursuant to section 2(a) of the Charter, and the equivalent provisions in human rights legislation.

The Ontario Court of Appeal set the standard for dismissal for denominational cause in *Re Essex County Roman Catholic School Board and Porter et al.*[38] The court stated that because the constitution allows for denominational schools, and schools generally can dismiss for cause, denominational schools may dismiss for denominational cause. This reasoning was adopted by the Supreme Court of Canada in *Re Caldwell et al. and Stuart et al.*[39] where the court upheld the dismissal of a teacher who had become pregnant while unmarried. The principles enunciated in those cases were also recently followed by the Newfoundland Court of Appeal in *Walsh v. Roman Catholic School Board for St. John's.*[40] The Newfoundland court made it clear that, provided a school board explicitly identifies that adherence to the basic tenets and philosophy of the particular denomination is a condition upon which employment is being offered, and that any breach of the condition will result in termination, a dismissal for breach is justified.

The Supreme Court of Canada has recognized the balancing necessary when dealing with these inherently contradictory rights but has fallen on the side of protecting the distinct nature of denominational schools:

> It is my opinion that, viewed objectively, having in mind the special nature and objectives of the school, the requirement of religious conformance including acceptance and observance of church rules regarding marriage is reasonably necessary to assure the achievement of the objectives of the school.[41]

The basic principle derived from this decision is that, where the actions of the teacher in a denominational school can reasonably be seen to undermine the religious objectives of the school, the teacher may be dismissed for cause. In some provinces, this rule has been specifically adopted in the education act.[42] Consequently, all teachers in denominational systems must be particularly careful in both their in-school and out-of-school conduct. There are obviously severe restrictions on privacy and lifestyle rights in cases where teachers are employed by denominational school systems.

Labour Law

Teachers are in a unique position in the field of labour law because the "public service" nature of their work has led to their collective bargaining rights and right to strike being more strictly regulated by statute.[43] The Supreme Court of Canada has decided, in a trilogy of cases outside education, that the Charter of Rights does not protect the right to strike or to collective bargaining.[44] There is, therefore, little room for teachers to argue that these legislative provisions are fundamentally unconstitutional. They are, consequently, left with more traditional remedies through labour law channels.

The collective agreement between school boards and teachers will be the guide for determining the rights and responsibilities of teachers including when they can strike. One interesting recent development in this area is the courts' protection of the right of teachers *not* to strike, pursuant to the teachers' association legislation. The courts in Newfoundland[45] and Quebec[46] have both held that the teachers' unions cannot discipline or suspend teachers who refuse to participate in these strikes.

The other important labour law issues for teachers are suspension and dismissal. It is well established that school boards have the right to suspend teachers with or without pay.[47] The critical question here is: what constitutes just cause for suspension or dismissal of teachers? Statutes sometimes provide guidance on the question, but it is most frequently determined on a case-by-case basis.[48] Another important issue is whether the teacher receives proper procedural protection before he or she is suspended or dismissed.[49] We will discuss proper procedural protection in more detail in the following section.

In terms of labour law, there is an additional danger for teachers lurking in the sections of the Criminal Code. If they are accused of an impropriety under the Code (particularly sexual interference or sexual touching), they can be subject to dismissal for cause even if they are acquitted of the criminal charge. A school board does not have the same criminal court restrictions of being satisfied "beyond a reasonable doubt" before acting to dismiss the teacher. The school board may set its own standard of proof, which is generally known as a "balance of probabilities." Put simply, this means that if the school board is convinced that a teacher more likely than not was involved in an impropriety with students, the teacher may be dismissed.

The B.C. case *Gallant v. Board of School Trustees of School District No. 61 (Greater Victoria)*[50] provides a good example of this process. In this case, the teacher was charged with a criminal offence of sexual assault on a 13-year-old youth. This case arose prior to the amendments to the Criminal Code in 1988. The school board suspended the teacher when the criminal charges were laid. Following his acquittal, the teacher demanded reinstatement and repayment of lost salary. In reply, the school board ordered a new suspension based on "misconduct." The B.C. legislation provided for a suspension of a teacher without pay for (a) misconduct, neglect of duty, or refusal or neglect to obey a lawful order of the board; or (b) where the teacher has been charged with a criminal offence and the board believes the circumstances created by it render it inadvisable for him or her to continue his or her duties.

The teacher challenged the legality of this second "revised" suspension and further challenged the dismissal on the same set of circumstances. The Supreme Court of British Columbia held that a school board is entitled to proceed under either reason for suspension, depending on the circumstances. The board is not prevented from suspending for misconduct where a teacher has been previously suspended and then acquitted of a criminal charge. The court specifically identified the test for a suspension for "misconduct" as that of a balance of probabilities whereas a suspension for a criminal conviction required that a teacher be guilty as charged beyond a reasonable doubt. A school board may proceed under one type of suspension and later proceed under the other type of suspension.

In another recent case in Saskatchewan,[51] the Court of Appeal examined a similar situation where a school teacher was tried and acquitted of a charge under the Criminal Code of sexual touching of some of his pupils under the age of 14 years. The judge made findings of credibility at trial that resulted in the acquittal. After the acquittal, the school division terminated the teacher's employment on the grounds that he had not "related with pupils in a manner satisfactory to the board" and that he had "failed to maintain the confidence and support of a significant number of parents of pupils." The matter went to a board of reference and before any hearing, the teacher made an application to have the board of reference determine what weight, if any, was to be given to the acquittal of the teacher in the courts. The board held that the fact of the acquittal would be considered with all other relevant facts but it was not *prima facie* evidence that in any way limited or restricted the evidence that could be called. The trial judge dismissed the teacher's application for review and the appeal court dismissed the appeal. The appeal court held that the ruling by the board of reference with regard to weight was clearly within the jurisdiction of the board to make and was not subject to judicial review. There is an alternative statutory route of appeal that was not pursued by the teacher and, therefore, this case may not yet be closed.

In another B.C. case,[52] a teacher was successful in avoiding dismissal where there were allegations of sexual misconduct. In this case, the teacher had a brief sexual encounter with an 18-year-old grade 10 student at another school. The young woman had been a student of the teacher when she was 16. The events allegedly occurred in 1985 and there were no criminal charges laid. The school board dismissed the teacher and the dismissal was upheld by a board of reference. The B.C. Supreme Court allowed an appeal from the board of reference decision stating that the dismissal was overly harsh in the circumstances. The B.C. Court of Appeal upheld the trial decision to replace dismissal with suspension on the basis that there was no risk of a repeated offence and that the incident was not related to the teacher-pupil relationship. The court, however, did state that since 1985, the attitude of society has changed greatly with respect to all aspects of sexual abuse. Much higher standards have been imposed on all persons involved in the teaching and child-care professions. Conduct that might have called for suspension in 1985 might well call for dismissal in 1987. That is certainly true for the 1990s.

In another case, a teacher who had been employed at a school board for 21 years was dismissed when he engaged in consensual sexual intercourse with a 17-year-old student. The board's decision was appealed to a judge of the Alberta Queen's Bench acting as the board of reference. At the time of the board of reference hearing, the teacher was living with the student. In upholding the termination, Justice Feehan stated:

> It would be wrong of [the school board] to send a message to teachers that they can expect anything less than *instant dismissal* if they engage in sexual activities with their students. Parents have the right to expect that they can continue to send their children to school without fear that they will be treated in such a manner.[53]

It is obvious from these cases that teachers must truly avoid any sexual contact with students. Even where the teacher has not been charged with any criminal offence, school boards have consistently taken the position that dismissal is the appropriate measure and the courts have upheld this position. Of course, any criminal conviction involving sexual conduct can also result in dismissal at the discretion of the board. The courts have consistently upheld the right of the school board to dismiss teachers where there has been a criminal conviction.

Although there is a focus on sexual offences primarily resulting in dismissal, there have been cases where other types of criminal charges have resulted in termination. Most education acts provide that a criminal conviction is cause for dismissal where the circumstances of the offence render it inadvisable to continue the employment of the teacher. In Manitoba, a teacher pleaded guilty to 11 charges of theft and one charge of public mischief. The criminal acts were admittedly the result of a mental illness suffered by the teacher. The teacher had an unblemished record as an exemplary teacher for 13 years with the school board; however, the school board elected to terminate the teacher on the basis of the criminal convictions. This dismissal was overturned by an arbitration board that accepted mental illness as a reason for abnormal conduct. The Manitoba

Court of Appeal overruled the arbitration board and reinstated the dismissal. The Court of Appeal decided that the school board, in fact, had cause for dismissal and it was not for the arbitration board to substitute their opinion of what the proper discipline should have been in the circumstances.[54]

The ramifications of sexual misconduct do not necessarily end at dismissal from a particular school board. Such misconduct may also result in a permanent revocation of one's licence to teach. In *Hansen v. The Disciplinary Hearing Subcommittee of the College of Teachers and the Council of the College of Teachers*,[55] the B.C. Supreme Court was asked to review the decision of the discipline committee who found a teacher guilty of misconduct for inappropriate touching of several students. The court declined to interfere with the decision of the discipline committee where the findings were largely based on credibility and the members of the committee were in a better position to assess the credibility of witnesses in the actual hearing. The teaching profession acts in every province entitle discipline committees to make findings of misconduct in cases where these findings are warranted.

Procedural Rights

Thus far we have concentrated on the "substantive rights" of teachers; however, no less important are the "procedural rights" of teachers. These rights apply to the manner in which teachers are treated by their employers and professional organizations. This area generally involves questions of whether the teacher was given an adequate opportunity to be heard and to respond to prejudicial evidence when subjected to disciplinary action. Procedural protections have traditionally been grounded in principles of administrative law. More recently, however, they have been derived from section 7 of the Charter.

Administrative law requires that government officials, and their delegates, provide certain procedural safeguards to individuals when decisions are made that affect the individual. Because education is regulated by the government, these protections must be extended to teachers. This means that teachers are entitled to a fair hearing and natural justice when they are suspended or disciplined. It may also arise where certification is at issue. In *Re Evershed and the Queen in Right of Ontario et al.*,[56] a teacher was convicted of unlawfully importing pornography into Canada and was dismissed by the school board. In addition, the minister of education, after reviewing the facts admitted at the criminal trial, decided to revoke the teacher's teaching certificate. This was challenged because the teacher was not given the opportunity to make representations to the minister before she made her decision. Even though there was a route of appeal to an advisory council, the decision of the minister was overturned by the court and the teacher was reinstated (with three years' back pay).

These same protections are offered to teachers in suspension and dismissal situations. Generally, school boards are required to develop evaluation procedures that contain teaching guidelines, provide for notice in cases where problems arise, provide for warnings, an opportunity for improvement, and finally some form of meeting with the employer, before a teacher can be suspended.[57] If the end result is dismissal, a further appeal is available through the grievance process in the collective agreement. Teachers' associations also have a responsibility to meet these standards when dealing with their members because employment is conditional on membership in the association. In *Forde v. O.S.S.T.F.*,[58] a principal challenged a two-year suspension by the teachers' federation for alleged unprofessional conduct. The principal was reinstated by an order of the court on the basis that he was not properly accorded the right to be heard and the opportunity to respond to complaints before he was suspended.

Two recent court decisions have opened up further means of protecting procedural rights for teachers through section 7 of the Charter. In the early years of Charter jurisprudence, this section was interpreted not to protect economic or employment rights. Therefore, if a teacher's employment was affected through suspension or dismissal, there was no protection under this section. In *Robert Olav Noyes v. Board of School Trustees, Dist. No. 30 (South Caribou)*,[59] for example, a teacher was suspended without pay after he was charged with a criminal offence, but before trial. The teacher claimed that his suspension violated section 7 as well as section 11(d) (presumption of innocence) of the Charter. The court held that "life, liberty and security of the person" did not include "employment." The court further held that the suspension did not presume guilt on the part of the teacher and, therefore, upheld the school board decision.

The B.C. Court of Appeal has more recently held, however, that section 7 of the Charter may be interpreted to protect employment rights under the term "liberty."[60] This case arose when doctors had restrictions placed on their practice by the provincial medical services commission, and the court decided these restrictions unduly fettered the doctors' rights to pursue their profession. In another recent case decided by the Supreme Court of Canada,[61] the court commented on the evolution of section 7 and indicated that the scope of the phrase "life, liberty, and security of the person" is broad enough to protect economic rights given the proper fact situation. This has yet to be tested in a teacher dismissal case.

Sexual Harassment

The problems of sexual harassment in the workplace have no doubt been occurring in schools for many decades. It is, however, only now becoming more common for complaints to be raised. The publicity of the Anita Hill and Justice Thomas confrontation in the U.S. Senate judicial confirmation hearings in the fall of 1991 catapulted the issue of sexual harassment to the forefront of the public agenda. The issue of sexual harassment is dealt with in Canada through the human rights codes and tribunals in each province. The case law has developed a position that "sexual discrimination" includes sexual harassment and employers have been subjected to review on the basis of that interpretation. However, modern human rights codes are being amended specifically to address the problem of sexual harassment. The recently redrafted Nova Scotia Human Rights Code provides:

> Section 5(2) — No person shall sexually harass an individual ...
>
> Section 3(o) — "Sexual harassment" means
> (i) vexatious sexual conduct or a course of comment that is known or ought reasonably to be known as unwelcome,
> (ii) a sexual solicitation or advance made to an individual by another individual where the other individual is in a position to confer a benefit on, or deny a benefit to, the individual to whom the solicitation or advance is made, where the individual who makes the solicitation or advance knows or ought reasonably to know that it is unwelcome, or
> (iii) a reprisal or threat of reprisal against an individual for rejecting a sexual solicitation or advance.

This provision and others like it will make it clear that "vexatious sexual conduct" or unwelcome sexual comments are now prohibited by law and subject to censure by human rights tribunals. There is also a right of redress for teachers where the unwelcomed conduct is that of another teacher or a school principal. The teacher may approach the school board to have the individual disciplined. The Supreme Court of Canada has held that employers are liable under human rights codes for the human rights violations of their employees particularly with regard to sexual harassment.[62] This reasoning has been specifically adopted and applied by the courts in relation to universities and there is no reason to believe that the same reasoning would not apply to school boards. Consequently, school boards have a crucial interest in maintaining tight controls on sexual harassment in the school environment and in taking appropriate action when a complaint is brought to their attention. We recommend that they adopt preventive measures against sexual harassment. If the school board's actions are viewed as insufficient, the complainant has the option of going to the provincial human rights commission.

One example of a school board taking action to address a complaint is found in the case of *Avalon North Integrated School Board v. The Newfoundland Teachers' Association*.[63] In this case there were complaints of sexual harassment brought by two teachers against the principal of their school. It was alleged that the principal put his arms around the teachers, and in one case touched the breast of one of the teachers. It was also alleged that he had pushed his body against one of the teachers, pressing her up against the wall, and that she was forced to push him away. The school board determined that a penalty of a one-year suspension and counselling was the appropriate discipline in the circumstances. The arbitration board held that the principal's behaviour was culpable and deserving of a major suspension; however, they reduced the length from one year to eight months. The arbitration board was mildly critical of the school board for not having an explicit policy on sexual harassment in the workplace.

The issue of sexual harassment is always a difficult one for the individual faced with the harassment. It is often a traumatic and disturbing situation. All teachers should be aware that there are real avenues for redress in cases where there is conduct sufficient to warrant a harassment complaint. A teacher may bring the complaint directly to the school board or to the local human rights commission. It is certainly advisable for school boards to develop policies and procedures on sexual harassment in the workplace and for teachers to take part in this process so that these situations can be avoided if possible, and dealt with properly when they arise.

Summary

It is clear that the rights and responsibilities of teachers, like all areas of education law, are in a process of revision to take account of the Charter of Rights. It will be up to the courts to determine the extent to which the Charter will affect the established practices, and how much weight will be given to court interpretations under the various provincial human rights codes existing prior to the Charter's enactment. One thing is clear: the law can be used to advance the rights of teachers as well as to enforce their responsibilities with respect to their employers, parents, and students.

ENDNOTES

1. In some rare cases a defendant has been ordered to comply with the Act in more substantive fashion. For example, in *Re Saskatchewan Human Rights Commission et al. and Canadian Odeon Theatres Ltd.* (1985), 18 D.L.R. (4th) 93 (Sask. C.A.), a theatre was ordered to make better space available for patrons in wheelchairs.

2. For a more complete discussion of the workings of human rights tribunals see Jane Price, *Teaching Human Rights: A Casebook for Senior High Teachers* (Halifax: Public Legal Education Society of Nova Scotia, 1988), at 11-23.

3. There is a Canadian Human Rights Act, R.S.C. 1985, c. H-6, which has a limited application to matters exclusively within federal jurisdiction (for example, national defence).

4. *Irwin Toy v. Quebec (Attorney General)* (1989), 94 N.R. (2d) 167, at 211 (S.C.C.).

5. *Keegstra v. Board of Education of Lacombe No. 14* (1983), 25 Alta. L.R. (2d) 270 (Board of Reference).

6. This is the American test for determining the limit on freedom of expression for students in school: *Tinker v. Des Moines Independent Community School District*, 21 L.Ed. (2d) 733 (U.S.S.C. 1969). See the discussion of this test in Chapter Two.

7. *David Attis v. Board of School Trustees, District 15 and Human Rights Commission and Malcolm Ross et al.* (1991), *School Law Commentary*, Case File No. 6-2-1 (N.B. Bd. of Inquiry).

8. The "gag order" originally placed on Mr. Ross by the Human Rights Board of Inquiry was lifted on appeal to the New Brunswick Court of Queen's Bench: see *Ross v. New Brunswick School District No. 15*, [1991] N.B.J. No. 1118 (N.B.Q.B.).

9. *Re Board of Education for the City of Hamilton and Ontario Public School Teachers' Federation* (1984), 13 L.A.C. (3d) 27. In this case the teacher not only criticized the employer, but refused to carry out instructions from the principal as part of the criticism. The teacher was removed from his teaching duties.

10. However, the school board may certainly try to keep the teacher in line: see the American decision *Pickering v. Board of*

Education of Township High School District 205, Will County, Illinois, 391 U.S. 563 (1968).

11. *Fraser v. Public Service Staff Relations Board,* [1985] 2 S.C.R. 455. See also S. Stushnoff, "The Freedom To Criticize One's Employer," in W.F. Foster, *Education and Law: A Plea for Partnership* (Welland: Editions Soleil Publishing Inc., 1992), from C.A.P.S.L.E. '90 Conference in Vancouver, B.C.

12. Regulation R.O.C. 437/85, made pursuant to The Teaching Profession Act, R.S.O. 1980, c. 495.

13. *Cromer v. British Columbia's Teachers' Federation and Attorney General of B.C.* (1986), 4 B.C.L.R. (2d) 273 (C.A.).

14. G. Dickinson and A.W. MacKay, *Rights, Freedoms and the Education System in Canada* (Toronto: Emond Montgomery, 1989).

15. If any activity that conveys meaning can be defined as "expression" (see *Irwin Toy,* supra endnote 4), then individuals could be seen to express themselves in their lifestyle.

16. *Abbotsford School District No. 34 v. Shewan and Shewan* (1986), 70 B.C.L.R. 40 (S.C.), appeal dismissed by Court of Appeal, December 21, 1987; leave to appeal to the Supreme Court of Canada denied June 30, 1988.

17. See, for example, *Kuschminder v. Sturgeon School Division No. 4* (1988), *School Law Commentary,* Case File No. 3-4-2 (Alta. Bd. of Ref.), where a principal was dismissed after pleading guilty to sexually assaulting a former student.

18. In a pre-Charter case, *Beckwith and Allen v. The Colchester-East Hants Amalgamated School Board* (1977), 23 N.S.R. (2d) 268 (T.D.), two teachers were dismissed because of their conviction for possession of marijuana.

19. See, for example, the provisions of the Nova Scotia Education Act and the Ontario Education Act set out in Chapter Two.

20. The sexual orientation of teachers is a matter of concern to many school boards and parents but under many human rights codes discrimination on the ground of sexual orientation is forbidden.

21. *Jamieson v. A.G.B.C.* (1971), 21 D.L.R. (3d) 313 (B.C.S.C.).

22. *Re Tomen and Federation of Women Teachers Association et al.* (1987), 61 O.R. (2d) 489 (H.C.J.).

23. This case has an interesting history. The O.P.S.T.F. used to be called the Ontario Public School Men Teachers' Federation; they changed their name to allow membership of both men and women. However, the womens' federation resisted this membership.

24. R.S.O. 1990, c. T.2.

25. *Lavigne v. Ontario Public Service Employees Union et al.* (1989), 31 O.A.C. 40.

26. See the discussion of section 15 in Chapter Two.

27. See *McKinney v. University of Guelph et al..* (1990), 118 N.R. 1 (S.C.C.).

28. *Ontario Human Rights Commission v. Etobicoke,* [1982] 1 S.C.R. 202, at 208.

29. In Canada: *Pacific Western Airlines v. Canadian Airline Flight Attendants Association* (1987), 28 L.A.C. (3d) 291; and *Centre D'Accueil and Sainte-Domitille v. Union des Employees de Service Local 298,* cited in (1989), *School Law Commentary,* Case File No. 4-1-1. In the United States: *Chalk v. U.S. District Court Central California,* 840 F.2d 701 (9th Cir. 1988). For a detailed discussion of AIDS-related discrimination and employment, see D.J. Jones and N.C. Sheppard, "AIDS and Disability Employment Discrimination in and beyond the Classroom," in *The Dalhousie Law Journal,* vol. 12, no. 1 (April 1989), at 103.

30. For a more thorough description of the chronology of events in this case, see Jones and Sheppard, ibid., at 103-4.

31. See William F. Foster, *The Canadian School Executive* (October, 1987), vol. 7, no. 4, at 3.

32. *Nevio Rossi v. School District No. 57* (1985), 7 C.H.R.R. decision 511 (B.C. Human Rights Council).

33. It will be easy for school boards to hide gender discrimination by simply claiming that the applicant is not qualified: see *Marie Furlong-Bass v. Deer Lake Integrated School Board* (1985), 6 C.H.R.R. decision 418.

34. *Brooks v. Canada Safeway Ltd.* (1989), 59 D.L.R. (4th) 321 (S.C.C.).

35. *Alberta Hospital Ass'n v. Parcels,* unreported decision, April 1992 (Alta. Q.B.).

36. The Ontario Court of Appeal in *Re Essex County Roman Catholic School Board and Porter et al.* (1978), 21 O.R. (2d) 255 stated that since the constitution allows for denominational schools, and schools generally can dismiss for cause, then denominational schools can dismiss for denominational cause.

37. The Newfoundland Court of Appeal has recognized the importance of section 29 of the Charter in upholding the right to dismiss

for denominational cause: *Walsh v. Federation of School Boards of Newfoundland* (1988), 71 Nfld. & P.E.I.R. 21.

38. *Essex County Roman Catholic School Board*, supra endnote 36.

39. *Re Caldwell et al. and Stuart et al.* (1984), 15 D.L.R. (4th) 1 (S.C.C.).

40. *Walsh*, supra endnote 37.

41. *Caldwell and Stuart*, supra endnote 39.

42. For example, Ontario's Education Act, R.S.O. 1990, c. E.2, section 136(1), which allows separate schools to require, as a condition of employment, that teachers agree to respect the "philosophy and traditions of Roman Catholic separate schools in the performance of their duties."

43. This is true of every province except Quebec.

44. *Public Service Alliance of Canada v. Canada* (1987), 75 N.R. 161 (S.C.C.); *Reference Re Compulsory Arbitration* (1987), 74 N.R. 99 (S.C.C.); *R.W.D.S.U. Locals 544, 496, 635, 955 et al. v. Saskatchewan et al.* (1987), 74 N.R. 321 (S.C.C.).

45. *Re Andrews and Newfoundland Teachers' Association* (1984), 47 Nfld. & P.E.I.R. 266 (Nfld. Dist. Ct.).

46. *West Island Teachers' Association et al. v. Madelaine Nantel et al.* (1988), 16 Q.A.C. 32. It should be noted that the trial division in this case raised the issue that the strike may have been called illegally.

47. *Re Board of Education for City of Hamilton*, supra endnote 9.

48. *Abbotsford School District*, supra endnote 16.

49. *Cardwell v. Board of School Trustees of School District No. 80 (Kitimat) and Attorney General for B.C.* (1985), *School Law Commentary*, Case File No. 1-5-5 (B.C.S.C.).

50. *Gallant v. Board of School Trustees of School District No. 61 (Greater Victoria)* (1987), *School Law Commentary*, Case File No. 2-8-5 (B.C.S.C.).

51. *Laughlin v. Board of Education of Battleford School Division No. 58* (1990), 83 Sask. R. 74 (C.A.).

52. *Larry Peterson v. Board of Reference and Board of Trustees of School District No. 65 Cowichan* (1988), *School Law Commentary*, Case File No. 2-7-5 (B.C.C.A.).

53. *Shanahan v. Board of Trustees of Edmonton Public School District No. 7* (1988), *School Law Commentary*, Case File No. 3-4-3 (Alta. Bd. of Ref.).

54. *Greenway v. Seven Oaks School Division No. 10*, [1991] 2 W.W.R. 481 (Man. CA).

55. *Hansen v. The Disciplinary Hearing Subcommittee of the College of Teachers and the Council of the College of Teachers* (1991), *School Law Commentary*, Case File No. 6-1-5 (B.C.S.C.).

56. *Re Evershed and the Queen in Right of Ontario et al.* (1984), 44 O.R. (2d) 763 (H.C.J.).

57. *MacDonald v. Red Deer County No. 23* (1986), 44 Alta. L.R. (2d) 134 (Bd. of Ref.).

58. *Forde v. O.S.S.T.F.* (1980), 115 D.L.R. (3d) 673 (Ont. H.C.J.).

59. *Robert Olav Noyes v. Board of School Trustees, Dist. No. 30 (South Caribou)* (1985), 6 C.R.D. 400.10-1.

60. *Wilson v. Medical Services Commission of British Columbia*, [1989] 2 W.W.R. 1 (B.C.C.A.) (leave to appeal to S.C.C. refused, November 3, 1988).

61. *Irwin Toy*, supra endnote 4.

62. *Robichaud et al. v. The Queen* (1987), 40 D.L.R. (4th) 577 (S.C.C.).

63. *Avalon North Integrated School Board v. The Newfoundland Teachers' Association* (1990), *School Law Commentary*, Case File No. 5-2-1 (Bd. of Arbit.).

Epilogue:
The Omni-Competent Teacher

Teachers play many different roles in modern society and their complex relationships with students, parents, fellow teachers, and school administrators have been further complicated by legal rules. In the days of the one-room school, the teacher was in a very real sense the delegate of the parents and in a fairly direct way was employed by them. The school trustees, composed of the parents in the community, would hire and fire the teacher and set the terms of employment. The range of jobs that the teacher was expected to perform included janitorial tasks such as keeping the fire going, medical tasks such as checking for contagious diseases, the administrative supervision of the school, and, of course, teaching students in a wide range of grades. Even in those less complicated days, teachers played many different roles — a fact that is reflected in some of the older education statutes.[1] However, there were very few laws that intruded into the daily life of the teacher.

Today's modern teacher is still expected to play a wide variety of roles — parent, educator, police agent, social worker, and nurse, to name but a few. There are also many different legal rules that structure and define the roles of the teacher in the modern school. As emphasized in the preceding chapters, the legal rights and responsibilities of the teacher depend upon the role that the teacher is playing at the relevant time. The *in loco parentis* role of the teacher has diminished and the teacher acts in various capacities as an agent of the state. Because the Charter of Rights only regulates state agents, the teachers' evolution from parental delegates to state agents has also swept them into the net of constitutional law. This, coupled with the growth of statute law, has plunged teachers into the legal dimensions of the educational process. Teachers sometimes feel as though they have been parachuted into a foreign land.

Although the arrival of the Charter in 1982 has been the major force in the judicializing of education, it is not the only one.

141

Education statutes and related regulations have become more detailed year by year and new laws regulating employment, medical practices, and child guidance have emerged. Judges and lawyers have become much more involved in educational policy making and there is a growing consciousness about the legal implications of being a teacher. There has also been a growing rights consciousness among both students and parents who look, with increasing frequency, to the courts to solve educational problems.[2] This does not mean that the courts are running Canadian schools. Indeed, the traditions of deference to local school boards and political authorities are still alive and well in Canada. Law has become a more vital aspect of education and crucial to understanding the roles of the teacher and the expectations placed upon him or her. Some understanding of the legal framework within which the teacher operates is essential to being a good teacher.

There are important debates about whether the growing role for lawyers in Canadian education is a good thing, but whatever the resolution of those debates, the reality cannot be denied. We live in a society that is increasingly regulated by laws and teachers, like everyone else, cannot escape this reality. Rather than decry this state of affairs, teachers are well advised to learn about the legal implications of their job and it is to that end that we have produced this book.

As the preceding chapters reveal, it is not possible to write about teachers and the law without also discussing the rights and responsibilities of the other actors in the field of education. In order to examine the rights of teachers in the workforce, we also explored the rights and duties of school boards and administrators in their role as employers. Only by understanding the rights of parents and students is it possible to get a fix on the legal role of the teacher in the school. Because the role of the teacher has grown, it is even necessary to have a glimpse at the role played in our society by the police, social agencies, and medical professions. Of course, it is also vital to re-examine the meaning of education and teaching.

The school provides a microcosm of the larger society and the value disputes inherent in it. Long before the Charter's enactment, the central Canadian issues of language, religion, and culture were being played out in the schools. Denominational education has been entrenched in the Canadian constitution since 1867 and, as we have seen, this limits the human rights of many Canadian teachers. Minority language educational rights were only entrenched in 1982 in section 23 of the Charter, but the emotional debates about this issue have much deeper roots. The education of Aboriginal children, a national disgrace, is only in the 1990s starting to get the attention it deserves. There is also a growing awareness that by imposing

Christian values in our schools we are pursuing a policy of cultural assimilation. This awareness is particularly important for teachers in recognizing the historic claims of First Nations people as well as the contributions of Canadians from many different ethnic backgrounds. Canada is truly becoming a multicultural society and this fact is little reflected in our schools. Indeed, one of the difficult challenges for teachers is the fight against the pernicious influences of racism in Canadian society.

In addition to these broad social and national challenges, the teacher is ultimately responsible for the education of children. Contrary to some of the bad press that teachers get, most teachers are dedicated people who care about the students that they teach. In some cases, the law appears to interfere with this expression of care, as is dramatically emphasized by the law on sexual interference. In other cases, the law imposes a legal duty of care in respect to negligence cases. To many teachers, the law and its complex rules are the enemies of education and harmonious teacher-student relations.[3] We do not agree. Lawyers and teachers can and must work together to provide a better education for students. Understanding the legal framework for schools is an important aspect of forming a constructive partnership that can serve the interests of all Canadians. The omni-competent teacher cannot ignore the law that has Lecome as much a part of the school environment as the air we breathe.

ENDNOTES

1. Education Act, R.S.N.S. 1967, c. 81, s. 54.

2. W. MacKay, "The Rights Paradigm in the Age of the Charter," in R. Ghosh and D. Roy, eds., *Social Change and Education in Canada* (Toronto: Harcourt Brace Jovanowich, 1991), at 202.

3. Dr. Ursula M. Franklin, in an address to the C.A.P.S.L.E. '92 Conference, suggested that the competition fostered by both lawyers and educators breeds violence. See *Education and the Law: The Partnership Grows* (Toronto: C.A.P.S.L.E. Conference, May 4, 1992). We agree that competition is fostered by both educators and lawyers and is at best a mixed blessing.